Christian Education Through the Church

FRANK M. McKIBBEN

Emeritus Professor of Religious Education
GARRETT BIBLICAL INSTITUTE

ABINGDON PRESS

New York   •   Nashville

CHRISTIAN EDUCATION THROUGH THE CHURCH

Library of Congress Catalog Card Number: 47-11950

J

SET UP, PRINTED, AND BOUND BY THE
PARTHENON PRESS, AT NASHVILLE,
TENNESSEE, UNITED STATES OF AMERICA

Dedicated To

CATHERINE (age seven) and DAVID (age one)
and their Generation

For whom ever more effective Christian
Nurture must be provided

A major purpose in writing this book has been to present something of a philosophy of religious education as it relates to the local church and to provide an overview of the program of religious education as it is worked out on the basis of this philosophy. It is the conviction of the writer that one of the main causes of the ineffectiveness of Protestant education has been the lack of such a philosophy or basic point of view and the fragmentary manner in which Christian education has been provided in the local church. Religious education as represented in the traditional Sunday school, or its modern successor the church school, has been thought of primarily as the "wing," or the "arm," or some other appendage of the church, not *the church itself, the total program of the church planned as an educational enterprise.* Not until recently have we developed an adequate approach to one of the most important concerns of each local church.

The church's program consists of the functions it is called upon to perform, the ministries it must render to its own constituency, its community, and the larger world. The educational program is not a segment or aspect of this larger program, but rather it consists of these functions carried forward as an educational enterprise. *Educational method is involved in all of them.* The principle of gradation has rightly become almost universally accepted in modern religious education. But such gradation has in turn contributed to the breakdown of the essential unity of the program and the constituency. A *functional* approach is made in this text. It addresses itself to the best ways of providing *all* the ministries of the church to its *total* constituency. Such ministries are usually provided in the end on a graded basis. But it is

7

believed that the manner of treatment here presented preserves the unity of both the program and the total membership of the church.

It will be readily recognized that the limitations imposed upon this book permit only a skeleton outline of the educational program of the church. But if ministers and leaders will think through their own educational work and develop it in harmony with the suggestions herein presented, they will, it is felt, be laying the foundations for an ever more effective program of Christian education in their churches.

FRANK M. MCKIBBEN

January 1, 1947
Evanston, Illinois

CONTENTS

CONTENTS

CHAPTER I

LOCAL CHURCH LIFE AND WORK

The group in the church conference room showed keen interest though the hour was late. The leader of the youth group had just finished an enthusiastic report on the past month's work. "We have our problems too," he concluded. "Not many of the older youth participate in the church service of worship on Sunday. We still need a good recreational leader for the Sunday evening and week time activities of our high school fellowship. And not all our teachers are satisfied with the way that they are handling their courses of study." Earlier in the evening the work with children had been considered. Various problems in connection with the adult groups had been discussed at the previous meeting. The minister had brought inspiration and help, not only in the devotional service he had conducted, but also by his constructive comments on various aspects of the program. Before adjourning they listed some of the problems that should engage their attention at the next meeting: the extent to which real evangelism was occurring among their youth and adults; causes of the low average attendance in the Intermediate department; the manner in which missionary training was being emphasized throughout the program; and participation of members of the group in the training class soon to be held. As they left the meeting those present had a sense of participating in an important enterprise. They constituted the

Church Board of Education. This was one of their regular monthly meetings.

Need of a Better Understanding.—Who of us does not feel keenly our need of better understanding of Christian education, although we may have been working in the church for many years? Marked progress has been made in this field in recent years. The older *Sunday School* has gradually been changed into the modern *Church School*. Now we are thinking and planning in terms of *the educational work of the church,* the entire program of the church planned and carried forward as an educational enterprise. We are concerned in this study, first of all, to gain an over-all picture of this larger educational program. Then on the basis of this we will consider the programs and methods by which Christian nurture may be provided for young and old.

How are we to begin our study of Christian nurture? Religious education gets its meaning from the Christian religion which it seeks to serve. Its purposes grow out of the church of which it is a part. It has to do with individuals and groups, therefore it must be planned so as to help develop Christian personalities and a more Christlike society. Education is central in the life and work of the church. It is *the* most important aspect of individual growth. Without it society cannot be made Christian. In order to understand Christian education properly we need to get an adequate interpretation of the Christian religion and the Christian church.

What Is the Christian Religion?—Our concern here is not with an extended discussion of religion, but rather with an interpretation that will lead us to a better understanding of Christian education. There are, of course, many different definitions of religion. It is impossible to find one that will meet the approval of everybody. We should be able to find commonly-accepted interpretations of religion within Protestantism. One of the simplest statements is this: religion is

12

man's effort to discover and do the will of God in all of life's relationships. Religion, according to one writer, "is man's life conceived and lived in relation to a world of a higher order, upon which he feels himself dependent, to which he knows himself under obligation, and in relation to which he finds life's meaning and seeks its completion." [1] This same writer defines Christianity as "the on-going life of that fellowship which has its origin and its abiding inspiration and guidance in Jesus. Christianity is Christ as the revelation of what God is and what man is to be. With reference to its central conviction, Christianity is the religion of redemptive good will; it believes in a God of creative good will; in the life of good will as the way for men, in the redemptive power of the spirit of good will working in and through men, and in the final triumph of that spirit in a coming rule of God." [2]

The common faith among Protestants may be found in publications of such agencies as the International Council of Religious Education and the Federal Council of Churches of Christ in America, which bring many denominations into cooperative activity. They find in these cooperating churches a common belief in God as the source of all existence. His ways are found in nature and within man through conscience. They believe that God's word has been proclaimed by the prophets and that in Jesus Christ God was made manifest in human life. It is their common belief that man is the child of God and that he attains his full stature only as the Spirit of God dwells in him. The central teaching of Christianity is the principle of love of God and love of fellowmen. It seeks to bring into fellowship all mankind, for all of whatever race or nation are children of God. [3]

Religion Involves Beliefs, Conduct, and Fellowship. —The Christian religion includes at least three things: (1) a faith, some definite beliefs; (2) a way of life, a mode of behavior; and (3) fellowship with God and with others.

13

Many efforts have been made to set forth the teachings of Jesus and the church. It would seem that this could be quite easily and simply done, and yet it is a matter over which heated conflict arises continuously. Individuals and groups differ radically in their understanding of what the teachings of Jesus mean and how beliefs about God and religion are to be stated. The religious leader needs to study this aspect of religion continuously in order to be clearer in his own mind and in order to be able better to interpret the teachings of religion to others. Fortunately each of us has the resources of centuries of Christian thought out of which to fashion his own beliefs. In some cases one's denomination has set forth its teachings in full and authoritative form.

Christianity involves *a way of life,* a type of behavior in harmony with these beliefs. One who professes to be a Christian should be characterized by certain attitudes, should manifest Christian virtues in daily conduct, should be moved to service in the spirit of Jesus Christ. These are the major tests of one's religion. "By their fruits shall they be known." Christianity undoubtedly makes the severest demands of its followers in their daily conduct of any known religion.

True religion creates *a fellowship* between the individual and the divine and kindred spirits. We need help in living the Good Life. It must be shared with others. We never get beyond the need of the stimulation and encouragement that comes from communion with our fellows. Christianity involves a rich living fellowship with God and with others. One of the unique forms this fellowship takes is that of group worship.

Christian education, therefore, is concerned to interpret to each generation this faith, this common body of religious teaching. It seeks to open up the Christian way of life and to lead people in effective living in that way. It attempts to bring young and old into vital relation to the fellowship of Christians, fellowship in daily living, worship of God and service to humanity. Thus it is seen how important it is for the leader and teacher of Christian education to seek an ever clearer, fuller understanding of what religion means.

What Is the Church?—There are in the United States, many millions of Protestants. All of them have some kind of a religious home, a local church, where their spiritual life is nurtured, where religion is interpreted to them, where they have fellowship with kindred spirits, where they worship, and where they are encouraged and given opportunity to serve. The Christian religion could not long survive without these local groups. As go the spiritual life and health of these religious groups, so for the most part will go the life of Christianity in the western hemisphere, and probably in the larger world.

These churches are located in an infinite variety of situations: slums, cultured suburbs, countrysides, industrial centers, barren plains, fertile valleys, and college campuses. Their physical resources mount into many millions of dollars. Many different types of people are attracted to their life and ministry. They maintain a constantly broadening program. They hope ultimately to evangelize the uttermost parts of the earth. The church with all its defects and limitations has been and still is a mighty force in the life of the world.

But whatever the church is in its broader aspects, it is in the last analysis the comparatively small fellowship of adults, youth and children who constitute the local church. It is here primarily that the Christian religion has its roots and finds expression in life, in personalities enriched and transformed, in services rendered, and in material resources developed. It is small wonder, then, that repeated efforts are made to strengthen and make more effective the life and work of these local churches.

But what is the church? We are confronted by a wide

15

variety of interpretations. The church, like all other institutions in society, has grown up in the course of human history. And yet it has always been claimed that the church is more than the mere product of human development. It is considered to be the "representative of God in the world"; it is the "bride of Christ," spiritual and invisible, yet sustaining a real life on earth. It is believed to be of this world yet beyond it, a communion of saints that extends back to the beginning of time and on to its end, a spiritual fellowship of all those who have found their life with God.

We are, however, in the last analysis always concerned with the local church as we find it in our communities. Whatever may be its divine origin and nature, it is essentially human, made up of people living, working, suffering, and achieving in the here and now. Whether or not it is the "body of Christ," it most surely is an institution alongside many other agencies in a rapidly changing complex society. Whether or not it is a "communion of saints through endless time," it is decidedly a fellowship of Christians in the here and now attempting to express in their individual and corporate lives the will of God and the teachings of Jesus. Whatever measure of the "grace of God" is vouchsafed to the fellowship, it is necessary for it to plan activities, develop leadership and set up an effective organization.

The church is a society of persons whose aim is "to secure within individuals and society an ever-increasing practice of the attitudes toward God and men that were revealed in the life and teachings of Jesus." [4] It is a religious community providing its members a firsthand experience in Christian living and opportunities to share in making the Kingdom of Love and Righteousness operative in the world about them. Conceived in its simplest terms it consists of a *life* and a *work*. It is *life,* a continuing experience of fellowship, worship, study, and service. It is a *work*. "My Father work-

16

eth hitherto, and I work," said Jesus. The church provides His followers opportunity to carry on the work begun by Jesus, that of realizing ever more perfectly the will of God among men.

The Specific Purposes of the Church.—Just how does a church do its work? This is best seen by an analysis of the main functions the church must perform if her task is to be accomplished. These functions may be variously stated.

The major functions of the church are suggested by the chapter titles of a recent book on the total church program:

1. Securing Commitment and Enlistment within Individuals.
2. Building them into the Fellowship.
3. Making them God-conscious through group and Private Worship and Inspiration.
4. Enlarging their Insights through Education.
5. Expanding their Powers through Stewardship.
6. Increasing their Effectiveness through Organization.
7. Securing the Tools for their Work.
8. Moulding them into a Community Force for Righteousness.
9. Broadening their Horizon to Include the World Task.
10. Developing their Cooperative Relations with all their Fellow Christians.[5]

The following analysis will serve our purpose in this study. It may be said that the function of the church is:

1. *To interpret religion,* through study classes, sermons, lectures, interest groups, literature, and such other means as will make the total constituency intelligent regarding religion and its meaning for all of life.

2. *To provide worship and training in the devotional life* through various kinds of worship services, devotional exercises, and training in worship for all the age groups in the church.

3. *To promote and enrich the fellowship of Christians* through every means available and for all ages. Among the

17

means of providing this fellowship and enriching the lives of the members, various kinds of recreational activity will be found very helpful.

4. *To extend the fellowship to include an ever-increasing number of people,* through recruiting, evangelism, missions, and similar activities. The Christian church cannot fulfill the commands of the Master "Love thy neighbor as thyself," and "Go ye into all the world, and preach the gospel to the whole creation," without continuous effort to bring others into the fellowship of the Christian community, both at home and abroad.

5. *To provide incentive, training, and opportunity for individuals to participate in efforts to improve society.* It is not enough for the church to win and transform individual lives. The social conditions adversely affecting the lives of people in society must be corrected. To lead individuals and groups to study social issues, to participate in practical welfare work, to engage in social action looking toward the improvement of society constitutes one of the major functions of the church.

6. *To aid individuals* through care for their physical needs, pastoral ministry, and such personal counseling as they may require in their infinite variety of needs.

7. *To enlist and train workers for the local church, community and world.* The local church has always been responsible for providing the leadership required to carry on its own program. In addition, it has been a continuous source of inspiration for workers in the various social, philanthropic, and civic activities of the community of which it is a part.

8. *To maintain a wholesome and effective institutional life.* The home base of Christianity is the local church. Unless it is well organized and capably administered, with its personnel and physical resources effectively handled, and through it all

a fine spirit of devotion and cooperation shown, the church will not be able to carry forward all the functions just listed.

What Is the Church Program?—If the purposes suggested are to be realized and these functions performed, some plan of procedure must be adopted. It involves a spread of activities and plan of human relations, and some form of organization. Most of us have been brought up in the church and are apt to assume that these activities and relationships just happen automatically. They do not. Someone must plan for them. Someone must administer them. Someone must evaluate and improve them. This is the process of program-building.

What goes on in the typical church? Let us take a look within an average fellowship. A complete list of the week's activities might fill several pages, but the following are suggestive: we will observe various worship services on Sunday; simultaneous class sessions of varied sizes and ages; informal devotional services during the week; missionary meetings of women on some afternoon; a boy's club meeting after school; a church board meeting some evening; a high school party on Friday night; a mothers' circle spending the afternoon in some home; a church office sending out literature and mail; a pastor making calls upon sick persons and maintaining hours for consultation in the church office; some teacher visiting a sick pupil; a small group of adults in a home discussing some social issue; and so on through the week. *This is church life and work!*

Such a "look in" seems to present a "hodgepodge" of activities. And sometimes it is just that! For often there has been little careful planning and slight concern for a well-rounded and effective program. But what should enter into the church's program? It is at this point that the complete list of functions just referred to gives direction. *A church program consists of all the activities, materials, resources,*

19

*physical facilities, and personnel involved in carrying forward
the full outline of functions.*

If we were to attempt to picture the program of the
church as we have just described it through an analysis

THE CHURCH

The Program should provide
Training—experiences
in

Worship		A	Y	C
Study-Interpretation		D	O	H
Fellowship-recreation			U	I
Evangelism		U	N	L
Missions			G	D
Stewardship	For	L	P	R
Social Education-Action		T	E	E
Counseling-Pastoral Care			O	N
Leadership Training		S	P	
Larger Church Relations			L	
Et cetera, Et cetera			E	

THE CHURCH

of its functions, it would probably look like the chart on this page.

It will be noted from the diagram that there is *one* church, not several different organizations each semi-independent of the others. Adults, children, and young people are considered as groups as a whole to receive the ministries of the total program. Thus the worship program of the church is not just the eleven o'clock preaching service, but all the worship services provided by the church to meet the needs of children, youth, and adults. This may mean one service each week; it may mean several, depending upon how the program is planned in the individual local church. This would be true for all elements in the program, instruction, fellowship, and the others suggested.

What Is Educational Method?—Ministers, workers and lay members of the church should be concerned to discover and use the most fruitful methods of bringing the life of the local fellowship to the richest and fullest expression and to the highest point of effectiveness in service. The ends which the church seeks, Christ-like persons and a Christian society, are so important and the resources at her disposal so limited that she dare not continue on a basis of partial success. There are ways *and* ways by which local church life and work are carried forward. Functions involve methods of performing them. Definite procedures and technics are used in every phase of the program. *Whatever contributes to successful work with individuals and to the effective direction of group life and action constitutes method.* In the broad and inclusive sense, *method is the creation and maintenance of conditions that promote individual and group growth.* These conditions are as varied as human experience; they relate to all forms of individual and group life and activity in the church. The list of functions or ministries just outlined constitute the major "sets of conditions" that must be provided and con-

21

trolled. All persons who are participating in any form of leadership or special service are concerned with method. They are seeking *the best ways* of making available the total resources of the Christian religion and the full ministries of the Christian church to all members within it. Thus it is that we are thinking more and more of Christian education as *the total program of the church carried forward as an educational enterprise*. The fuller interpretation of educational method will be the subject of the chapters that follow.

CHAPTER II

WHAT IS CHRISTIAN EDUCATION?

We have said that the purpose of the church is to bring about the development of Christ-like persons and a more Christian society. Christian education is primarily concerned with aiding in this process. All that enters into its procedures is designed to help individuals, young and old, to grow in Christlikeness and to aid in realizing the Kingdom of Love and Righteousness among men. Here is the ultimate test by which all forms of Christian education must be judged.

How Do Individuals Grow?—We may not have given much thought to the *way* in which growth actually takes place, and still less to *how* we actually influence that growth. Christian nurture has been interpreted to be a "reverent attempt to discover the divinely ordained process by which individuals grow toward Christlikeness, and to work with that process." [1] There are still many mysteries about the unfolding of personality, but most of us need to understand more fully than we do what is now known about growth and its control.

The first thing to note is that *growth occurs naturally and continuously.* If the individual is at all normal nature, or God, has provided for an inevitable maturing process. The body grows; it increases in size and new powers and abilities appear. The mind develops; its power of recollection, understanding and reasoning unfold. The social outlook and responses of the individual undergo change. Increasing social sensitivity and awareness accompany growth into adolescence

23

and adulthood. All of these elements of growth taken together produce what we recognize as the personality of the individual. The process is continuous. None of us remains the same. The body is undergoing steady change although growth in size may cease. The mind is acquiring new ideas and forming different attitudes, and the total personality is expressing itself in different forms of behavior. The process is very rapid during childhood and youth. It continues into adulthood. It should take place even to old age, although on a greatly lessened scale.

We may note also that while there are many factors that affect growth, two in particular are very important. One is the "stuff" the individual starts with, his native endowment, his inheritance. No two individuals are exactly alike. Basic differences spring in part from the inheritance received from the long line of ancestors each person has. Bodily size, foundations of temperament, and capacities for development are due largely to heredity, although we are still uncertain regarding the exact influence heredity has on individual development.

Growth Through Experience.—The other aspects of growth we are most concerned with, intellectual, emotional, social and spiritual, result largely from the experiences which make up the individual's existence. Our conscious life consists of a continuing stream of experiences. We are constantly reacting in some way to whatever presents itself in our environment. Hence the nature of our environment is exceedingly important. As teachers we can do nothing about the heredity of the individual. That has been settled long before we start to work with him. But all education is based upon the possibility of controlling the individual's environment and conditioning his responses to it. By the environment of a person is meant any objects and events, happenings, relationships, actions of other people, or what not that are present in his immediate neighborhood, and to which he is capable of responding in some manner. This interaction between the person and his environment makes up the continuing stream of experiences. It is through these experiences that changes are made in individual thought, feeling and action. Our concern is to bring about those changes that make the individual even more Christian in his thoughts, attitudes, and actions. Christian character grows as Christian attitudes and ideals come to dominate the whole round of daily living. You have doubtless heard the expression "experience-centered teaching" or "child-centered school." These terms grow out of the conviction that the all-important thing in educating a person is to aid *him* in having the right kind of experiences, that unless we are influencing the sort of experiences that make up *his* daily life we are not directing his education.

Learning on the part of the individual means actually making changes. Teaching then means seeing to it that persons have experiences that will bring about desirable changes. This we do in part by controlling the immediate environment, creating the conditions that are most apt to bring about these changes. Of course the person himself is not a passive but rather a most active factor in this changing process. His interests, abilities and past experience play a most important role. Sometimes it is impossible to lead growing youth into the actual experiences we want them to have. It frequently becomes necessary for them to share in the experience of others, parents, teachers, or those of past generations. We call this "vicarious experience," and it is very significant in all forms of education. It is for this reason that the Bible is so important in Christian education. It is full of the recorded experiences of people who have lived courageously, victoriously, and helpfully. We try to lead pupils into appreciation of the experiences prophets, saints, and heroes have had in the hope that they may themselves have something of the same kind of experiences as they grow.

Many Factors Influence Growth.—When growth and education are viewed in this light we see at once not only how continuous the development of the individual is, but also what a diversity of influences inevitably affect his life. "The social world in which we live is teaching the child continuously— in the home, on the street; through the newspaper, the radio, the motion picture show; through neighborhood gossip, narrow-minded parents, and prejudiced school books. The child is not only learning from the teacher but from the world, a world that teaches in season and out of season, directly and by implication, awards group conformity with social approval. ... For the educational process to make headway against the flood of influences which we have in our actual social customs the most direct effort must be exercised." [2] Thus it will be seen that a great variety of situations affect growth and that many of these influences lie outside the program and direction of the church.

We are now able to identify some of the major aspects of this growth process and how we may direct it. First, *growth takes place when the individual absorbs, assimilates, the life about him.* As we have noted, this process goes on continuously and spontaneously. We are all products of it. It means that the attitudes, habits, customs and practices of the group with which a person lives are usually taken over unconsciously and become his own. This is particularly true in the early years of life. The individual inevitably responds to the influence of those about him. Many of us were surrounded by religious influences from infancy. We cannot recall when we learned to pray. We unconsciously absorbed our parents' loyalty and devotion to the church. Their standards and ideals determined much of our daily conduct. The training received in this way when the child is inexperienced and his nature responsive stays with him throughout life. It is now generally recognized that more is accomplished in this way during the first five years of childhood than during any subsequent period of equal length. Hence it is that the church is becoming increasingly interested in parent education and is extending her formal program of religious nurture into the pre-school years. One of the most important elements in this form of growth is the response the individual makes to the love and affection received from those in the intimate family group. This is absolutely essential to proper growth, more important in the early years but something the need of which we never outgrow.

Second, *growth takes place through participation in the life and activities of the group.* This is simply a continuation of the process referred to above. As children grow older this participation becomes more conscious and meaningful. The individual learns to worship, to serve and to take part in all the activities that make up Christian living through sharing in them in whatever group he is placed. Children love to "have a part" in the activities of the home, the church and the school. In their play they dramatize many of the forms of the group life surrounding them. One reason this form of growth is so effective is that *individuals learn primarily by doing things* rather than by talking about them. Our concern as teachers is to make sure that the individual's responses to the situations life presents are of a high Christian character. We will be concerned to create an environment in which the growing individual *will learn the Christian way of life by living it.* This means that many situations need to be provided whereby growing persons will be led into intelligent and full participation in activities that are a concrete expression of Christianity.

The third process directly involved in growth is that of *thinking and reasoning.* This means the gaining of new

27

insights and meanings, the development of reason and creative imagination, and discoveries of truth and seeing its application to life. Each individual needs to develop the power of self-guidance, and he does this through facing actual life situations, through judging consequences, and choosing and working for ends in life that are in harmony with his ideals. He learns to use not only his own growing experience but also that of the past. All education contributes to this process. The concern of Christian education is to help the individual develop worthy purposes, acquaint him with the richness of past religious experiences, and to aid him in the use of the religious resources that are available to make life thoroughly Christian. This process cannot begin too early and it must continue to the end.

We will be concerned to help people face the actual situations life presents and to handle the issues according to Christian ideals and purposes. The high school boy who faces his first temptation to drink liquor, the girl who is tempted to repeat gossip that would seriously hurt a friend, the child who faces a temptation to do petty stealing, the adult who feels he cannot accept a person of a different race and color as a real friend, are facing situations where "thinking through" to religious conduct is involved. Others may help but final decisions are their own. Such situations range from the simple problems of childhood to the very complex and difficult ones of later youth and adulthood.

In the fourth place, *individuals grow religiously by committing themselves to great persons and causes.* Individuals must have someone or something to command their total loyalty. It is almost inevitable that growing persons will build their lives around some center of devotion. Such loyalty serves to organize the personality and gives power and direction to life that can come from no other source. For the growing Christian it means identifying oneself with the person of

Jesus Christ; it means commitment to the purposes of God as set forth in the teachings of Jesus; it usually involves assuming membership in the Christian church. It means willingness to stand up and be counted for "truth and righteousness" under all circumstances. For Christians the all-inclusive loyalty in life is religious, and there is no center of loyalty comparable to the God of Jesus Christ. One of the surest ways to promote one's religious development is to identify oneself with God's Kingdom of Love and Righteousness, to lose oneself in the unfinished task of this Kingdom. Few things will do more to integrate the life and enable one to discover his best self.

Growth Is Both Gradual and Uneven.—This process of development does not always take place in an even, gradual manner. There occur periods of special quickening of the spiritual life, moments of unusual feelings of weakness, guilt and frustration, times of vivid awareness of God's spirit, occasions when important decisions must be made. For those who have lived outside the fellowship of Christians, or whose lives have been out of harmony with the purposes of God, the experience of turning to God, accepting discipleship to Christ, joining the church, may be one of marked emotional intensity. Such experiences have usually been called "conversion." They are not contrary to the principles of Christian nurture, but represent different forms of adjustment the personality may undergo in religious development. The program of Christian education should provide abundant opportunity for people of all ages to enter into such experiences as are normal to their wholesome development. They do not necessarily require special evangelistic effort. They may occur naturally in worship services, personal counseling, class sessions, times of happy fellowship, the regular preaching service, or the youth fellowship meeting. This means that there need be no sharp distinction made between evangelism and Christian nurture. Evangelism worthy of support must be educational in nature. And no program of Christian education will be fully effective that is not evangelistic in spirit.

The Place of God in Education.—The interpretation just given should not be regarded as in any sense minimizing the activity of the Spirit of God in the growing process. A common criticism of religious education is that it "leaves God out." It is felt that there is an over-emphasis upon what the teacher does and neglect of the part of the Divine Spirit. It should be said at once that in this discussion *all consideration of method and procedure takes place on the assumption that there is a "background of Divine Grace."* Whatever part the human agent may have in the development of Christian character is accomplished not contrary to or apart from, but in cooperation with the work of God's Holy Spirit. Whenever an individual achieves a genuinely *good act* he has an experience of religion. God thereby becomes incarnate in the life of the person. God participates in the good act; He confirms the good act; He fellowships with the person in the outcomes of the good act. Character becomes religiously charged whenever individual experience rises to climaxes of self-achievement and self-identification with the good, the true, and the beautiful in any section of God's world. This quality of character may be cultivated through the ordinary programs of the family, club, camp, school, and church. We should help children to realize that these genuinely creative experiences are religious in nature; thus much of daily experience will take on sacred significance. In reality the religious leader is endeavoring to create at all times the conditions under which the individual may respond more fully to the influence of God's Spirit.

All that has been learned about successful work with individuals and about the operation of God's Spirit points to the fact that the Creator has planned that growth should take place according to laws of development. It is our concern to understand more fully these laws in order that cooperation with them may be more intelligent. We explore the psychology of the human organism to capture its secrets. We observe human behavior to learn its ways. We experiment and measure to master more fully the conditions affecting growth of human personality. But we do this in the full realization that in the last analysis God causes growth. God is the creative life force within the individual and He and He alone causes the individual to mature. All that man can do is to attempt to surround the person with those stimuli, conditions and influences which will best enable personality to come to its finest and fullest expression. We work with God's process of unfolding life, whether we teach, preach, counsel, guide home life or lead in worship. Education or teaching, broadly interpreted, consists of the *creation and maintenance of those conditions that promote individual and group growth.*

Education has to do with groups as well as with individuals. Groups as such can experience development. A club, a class, a worshipping congregation, or a youth fellowship may experience a strengthening of social solidarity, a growing ability to act as a group, an increasing awareness of true Christian fellowship, a more driving sense of group responsibility. Education has to do with giving direction to and making more meaningful these significant relationships of life. Individuals do not live in a vacuum. Most of the education and growth individuals experience occurs in connection with social groups. Those who give leadership in Christian education will be concerned to master the methods and technics of group work.

Creating Conditions of Growth.—We have already noted that educational leadership in the broadest sense consists in *creating and maintaining conditions that promote individual and group growth.* We have also seen that not all the conditions that affect the individual's reactions can be brought under control. The "conditions" which the educator seeks to control are greatly varied in character. They include those represented in the typical class session, the Boy Scout meeting, the personal conference, the hill-side devotional service as well as the meeting of the Church Board of Education, the church service of worship, the missionary meeting, and the carefully planned recreational gathering. Work with individuals includes the simplest contacts between persons, such as the common forms of friendship, as well as the more professional aspects of pastoral care, counseling and spiritual guidance. Work with groups is of both formal and informal types. Formal groups include public worship, lectures, sermons, banquets; the more informal club meetings, discussion groups, fellowship circles and recreational activities.

The specific conditions we seek to control include the physical seating, the manner of grouping pupils, the types of activity employed, the person-to-person relations, the kind of resources used, and a host of other factors that must be taken into account. For instance, the type of room and equipment vitally affects the kind of class work done. Or pupils do not get all they might from a class session, a worship service or a social gathering because of the "grading," that is, those thus brought together vary so greatly in age, interests, and abilities as to be unable to work together profitably. A group may attempt to worship under "conditions" noisy and confusing, or with a service carelessly thrown together, or with leadership unprepared and unskilled, and thus fail utterly to enter into an experience of worship. The *conditions* simply were not conducive to worship.

Skill in teaching and leading therefore consists of insights into and understanding of those "sets of condition" that affect the responses of people. It involves mastery of the procedures and materials by which those conditions are provided that are most conducive to the kind of response desired. It will be readily seen by this interpretation that *educational method applies to all aspects of the church's program.* We will recall the major functions the church must perform in carrying forward its full ministry: worship, interpretation of religion, fellowship, social service, evangelism, missions, stewardship, personal counseling, and leadership training. While these functions have much in common, each has its own "sets of conditions," methods, materials, personal relationships, physical requirements, and skills in leadership.

Many types of leadership are needed to care for the total program of the church. Teaching or group leadership is so complex a process, so varied in its forms and so rich in its possibilities, that it is almost impossible to describe and classify all the forms it takes. Skillful leadership grows out of a detailed study of the various methods by which development of individuals and groups is guided. The next chapter will deal with some of these methods in some detail.

Christian Experience the Final Goal.—In the last analysis it is what people *experience* that constitutes life and growth. In building program and exercising forms of leadership, our ultimate concern is that people be brought to experiences of one kind or another. We provide worship services in order to make more readily possible *experiences of God-awareness;* we study and plan social action programs so that individuals will actually *experience* different attitudes, appreciations, and the satisfactions of "doing something about it." We give them opportunity to play together, exercise leadership, acquire skills, which in the end are *experiences* that actually constitute growth and development. The final test of all that we do as teachers and leaders is: what is happening to people? What *experiences* are they actually having and what *changes* are taking place in their lives? Are these experiences Christian?

CHAPTER III

WAYS OF HELPING PERSONS GROW

A Youth Fellowship Meeting.—As the young people began to gather in the church parlor on Sunday evening, a small group in one of the classrooms was just finishing an hour's session. It was the cabinet of the fellowship. The president, a boy of seventeen, had been presiding. The group had reviewed the activities of the past month, suggestions for improvement had been passed upon, and plans for the next month had been outlined. The responsibility for conducting the evening meetings rested squarely upon the young people themselves. The adult counselor had kept in the background, offering suggestions only as seemed necessary.

The program for that evening began with a "sing" around the piano as the young people gathered. As they seated themselves informally about the room, two of their number led a discussion on "How can we be more Christian in dealing with the negro young people in our high school?" A large number of the young people participated. A lively discussion took place. This was followed by a brief devotional period centering in the same theme. Informal conversation occurred as light refreshments were served. Fun and fellowship prevailed as they sat about the tables, although some of the young people were still discussing the negro problem. No one seemed to be in a hurry to get away. The evening closed with some games.

Future leaders were in the making. The two adult counselors present *exercised skillful leadership* by staying in the background and permitting the young people to direct their own activities. Real leadership sometimes means just that! It consists primarily in creating the conditions wherein young people sense their own responsibility and meet it. Frequently a leader will need to encourage a timid youth, assist another in carrying out an assignment, or help the entire group get a sense of direction.

A Primary Group at Work.—Eighteen Primary children were busily at work. They had been greeted as they came into the room and many were the items of interest they had to report. As they placed their clothes on hangers there was excited conversation. Spring was "just around the corner." They gathered quickly about a plant in one of the windows that had during the week put forth a new bud. For this the children had waited for some time, and they alternated between cries of delight and moments of quiet wonderment. During one of these moments a teacher led them in a brief prayer of thanks to God for the new flower, after which they sang one of their favorite hymns. Informal discussion took place for a few minutes before the pupils went to their tables to finish projects they had started the previous Sunday.

During the rest of the session a story was told, they had a listening period as some of the group recalled scripture verses they had previously learned, they interpreted in drawings and cut-outs the story they had heard, and the period closed with a circle worship service. The teachers engaged in quiet conversation with the children as they put their materials away and got out their wraps. One of the teachers held an extended conference with a boy who had failed to enter into the activities.

Anyone observing the entire session would have noted the range of activities engaged in and the types of leadership required: fellowship, story, conversation, direction of creative activities, worship, and friendly counseling. While the activities seemed to move naturally from one thing to another, yet it was the leader who "set the stage," who "created the conditions," that prompted the children to engage in the desired activities. There was ample evidence of careful planning and skillful leadership.

Church Board of Education Meets.—The minister was presiding over the session of the Church Board of Education. Following a brief devotional service led by a member of the group, he presented an order of business which was adopted. Committee reports were acted upon and several miscellaneous matters were quickly disposed of. Then the main item of business was taken up. It was a consideration of how to create a more Christian attitude toward Japanese-Americans who had recently moved into the neighborhood against the vigorous protest of many people in the community, including members of the church. The minister had been asked to open the discussion. This he did by setting before the group several questions.

Do we need to begin with ourselves, our prejudices and actions? Do we all fully accept the principle of Christian brotherhood toward every race? What is responsible for unchristian attitudes toward the newly-arrived Japanese? How do we go about getting rid of prejudices in ourselves? In others? How may we deal more effectively with this problem in the various age groups in the church school? Shall this church go "all out" for the practice of Christian brotherhood toward all races? If so, how?

A lively discussion followed. At times it grew quite heated, but the minister was able to challenge them to a fair and objective attitude. After extended consideration he attempted to summarize the discussion by listing on the blackboard the following points: (1) They all seemed committed to the Christian conception of brotherhood toward all races. (2)

Most of them felt they themselves had not been willing or able actually to express such brotherhood toward all races (the discussion had turned in the direction also of the negroes in their community). (3) They were convinced that they needed to take more seriously the "how" of dealing with prejudices. (4) They felt that more definite steps should be taken to deal realistically with Christian brotherhood throughout their educational program.

They all realized that they were dealing with a most difficult problem and one that would require long time handling. Two committees were formed for further study and report. One was asked to bring to the group guidance in dealing with prejudices. The other was assigned the task of outlining steps for more effective teaching and practice of brotherhood throughout their educational program. These items were made the order of business for the next meeting. As the meeting closed several members complimented the minister on his tactful and effective chairmanship. This is a form of leadership ministers and others are frequently called upon to exercise and one in which skill is greatly to be desired. It is an important way of promoting growth.

Group Relations Are Essential.—In the average local church will be found church school classes, missionary groups, Boy Scouts, committees, devotional gatherings, a Primary department, social action conferences, women's societies, young adult fellowships, recreational groups—and so the list might be continued. All these groups are involved in the educational program. They constitute the manner in which the various purposes of the church are carried forward. They are the ways in which persons are helped to grow and learn. We are concerned in this chapter with *the ways of promoting religious development,* and with *types of leadership* involved in these educational activities.

One's happiness in life depends largely upon his having

37

wholesome relations with his fellows. The development of the individual is central in any program of religious education, yet it is largely through various kinds of association that most of this development takes place. Each person is greatly affected by the groups in which he most vitally moves and of which he is an integral part. Our attitudes, ideals, motives, and habits are continually being shaped through our interaction with others. We will recall from the previous chapter that among the processes through which religious growth takes place are "assimilation" and "participation." These occur in various groups, the family, the church, the club, the youth fellowship and such other forms as were listed above. Our earliest faith is "faith in some one else's faith," that of a parent, teacher, or other person respected and admired. Devotion and loyalty to Christ and the church are revealed to us, not primarily through words and teachings, but first through being with persons whose lives are influenced by such devotion. Our first appreciation of the satisfaction found in service is gained from observing people who are rendering such service and are happy doing so. These elements of growth inevitably call for some kind of human association.

Types of Leadership.—The art of leadership of groups therefore is most important in the work of the church. Skill in teaching and leading requires a knowledge of a wide variety of conditions and a mastery of the procedures, resources and technics involved in providing the kind of environment that brings about desired changes. Certain typical methods of classroom work are known to all of us, such as story telling, memorization, discussion, directed conversation, project activity, dramatization, the use of audio-visual aids and a number of others less frequently used.[1] Each method calls for certain skills in leadership and in the use of resources. Anyone working intimately with groups, young and old, will probably be called upon at times to use some if not all of these procedures. However, most of these methods have been associated with a rather narrow idea of education. Here we are concerned with the broadest possible conception of leadership. We are dealing with *all* the functions of the church. We are seeking the *most fruitful ways* of making Christian education effective.

Method as Cooperative Group Activity.—One of the most helpful ways of regarding much of the educational work of the church, of understanding the ways of influencing growth, is to think of it as *cooperative group enterprise*. The group, such as a class, committee, fellowship or recreational club, enters into the cooperative direction of its own activity. This process may be truly democratic and embraces many of the values of genuine Christianity. Such procedure places responsibility where it belongs, with the total group. It recognizes the significance of the individual and gives him a voice in determining his own participation. It enlists the talents and enthusiasm of members of the group. It places responsibility on persons and holds them accountable for meeting it. It employs not one but various procedures that enable the group to achieve its objectives. It demands much of the leader but gives him full opportunity to use all the skills and talents he possesses. It affords a real opportunity to unite the group in enjoyable creative fellowship and activity.

Cooperative group enterprise as a procedure is all the more significant in view of the fact that the church has depended so largely upon the telling-listening process. Protestants are habitually *listening*—listening to the sermon, the prayer-meeting talk, the lecture of the Bible class teacher, the program of the missionary society. We can "take it on the chin" in listening to an amazing degree, and often with little change being made in our attitudes and conduct. It is very doubtful if the telling-listening process creates the most fruitful condition for individual and group growth. Certainly it has great limitations.

Cooperative group activity such as we are considering here is designed to provide the most stimulating conditions for growth in every phase of the church's program. We observed it in operation in the activities reported in the opening of this chapter. It provides opportunity for actual participation in a wide variety of ways. It calls for group decision as to methods of working together. It demands real thinking on the part of all members. Its purpose in promoting growth is *to realize all the values possible for all persons present in every situation.* Once this method is fully understood by leaders it is gratifying to discover the variety of group activities that lend themselves to its use.

There are many forms of teaching-leading that seem to call for preparation and activity on the part of the leader alone. He is expected to "tell," to lecture, to present information. All education involves such leadership at times. But the church's program has relied all too heavily upon this process, from the preaching of the minister to the lecture of the church school teacher. There will always be occasions where such "telling" will be necessary. But the whole educational program of the church can be vitalized and made more dynamic and effective if it partakes of the nature of creative group procedure as described above. For many ministers, teachers and other leaders it will mean a different approach to their work. It will involve developing skills in a wide variety of forms of leadership and helping members of the church achieve ability to participate in a broad spread of activities.

Leadership Skills Required.—Whenever a leader works with and directs a group, whether it be a class, committee, worshiping congregation, youth fellowship, women's society, or other association, he must "set-conditions," handle the relations, activities, resources, in such a way as to enable the group to achieve its purposes and individuals to come to the richest, fullest expression. In this process he may use any one or several of the various traditional "methods" referred to above. They will be used to further the progress of the group or lead individuals into helpful activities. Sometimes a discussion will be in order, at other times a lecture will take place, creative projects of some kind will be engaged in or a service of worship will be planned and conducted. The co-operative method will call for the largest amount of self-determination by the group regarding the methods by which they will work.

Each of these leadership activities calls for specific insights and skills. For example, in order to "build fellowship in a group" a leader needs to know how (1) to get people acquainted easily, (2) to make them feel at home in the group, (3) to break down artificial barriers, (4) to recognize and use abilities of individuals, (5) to provide activities that engage the entire group, (6) to utilize small groups for developing intimate acquaintanceship and encouraging participation by shy people, (7) to arouse pride in group achievements, (8) to arrange sufficient meeting and continuous association to develop group feeling, and (9) to follow up absentees.

Or again, to lead a discussion one must know how (1) to help the group to define the topic or problem before them, (2) to break it down into specific topics or questions, (3) to set the limitations of the discussions, (4) to determine and help discover the kind of information to be secured, (5) to assign and motivate research and special preparation, (6) to keep the discussion moving and to the point, (7) to encourage participation among all members, (8) to summarize the discussion, and (9) to help determine the next steps for the group.

In chapters that follow we will take up some of the various elements that enter into the educational program, each of which involves a distinctive "set of conditions," such as worship with its unique physical setting, special devotional content, forms of participation, and skills in leadership. The same is true for the interpretation of religion or teaching, fellowship, social education and action, and the other functions of the church.

Person-to-person Relations.—Education inevitably involves close relations between a leader and members of a group. Such a person-to-person relation has been a major feature of Protestant education. In fact, the long-standing practice of the small class in the traditional Sunday school has been based upon the desirability of intimate association between the teacher and individual members of the group. The same is true of the youth group of the Sunday evening program and their adult counselor, as well as of numerous other associations in the church. Frequently the values possible in the small group have not been realized. But the principle of affording opportunity for the leader to become well acquainted with each person, learn of his interests, problems and needs and thus minister to him individually has long been accepted. Modern education and church work is recognizing this principle even more enthusiastically. This is seen in the greater emphasis upon personal counseling on all age levels. In the end nothing can take the place of friendliness, concern for an individual's welfare and help in times of difficulty and need. Such aid to individuals is more carefully planned for and more effectively followed up now than previously. While counseling may occur in an elementary manner with any teacher or leader, professional training in such forms of human relations is being sought by many ministers and other workers in the church. Such person-to-person relations constitute important "conditions" that promote the religious development of persons.

Other Important Factors.—Other important "sets of

conditions" must be controlled if the work is to be successful. Church school work has long suffered seriously from inadequate *housing and equipment*. Minimum essentials should be considered in attempting to improve the program. These include wherever possible rooms of suitable size for the group and activity involved; complete segregation for class and worship sessions; simple but appropriate equipment, varying according to the age and type of program; adequate space, light, ventilation, and attractiveness of decoration.

Frequently failure characterizes the activities of a given group because people are brought together who have widely varying interests and needs. This is the problem of *gradation*. The more immature the individuals are, the greater these differences are. Children need a high degree of gradation for most of their activities. Many youth groups encounter difficulty because they include young people of different ages. The older youth do not want the "kids" around, and the intermediates do not feel "at home" with those older. The desirability of segregating young adults for part of their program is commending itself. On the other hand, modern religious education has probably carried gradation to an undesirable extreme. The family is a primary unit for religious nurture. Children and their parents can profitably share in more activities in the church than has been commonly thought. More activities embracing the entire family are finding their way into the program of the church.

One of the serious handicaps of church work has been the limitations of *time*. The church school hour is all too brief, and is frequently cut even shorter by failure to begin on time and tardiness of pupils. While every effort should be made to conserve and use properly the time on Sunday morning, there is growing realization that the program should be greatly extended beyond this time. In some cases more time is made available on Sunday morning, especially for younger groups.

Increasingly question is being raised over the wisdom of taking time in the church school hour for worship for young people and adults who will have adequate opportunity to worship in the regular church service. Might not the time be better spent in longer class sessions? The Sunday evening is coming into greater use with youth and adults for various educational purposes. Fuller use of week days and nights for additional sessions is also indicated. Weekday religious classes, vacation schools, camps and institutes represent other ways of making more time available. Many other factors that affect the success of the program will need to be identified and dealt with if real effectiveness is to be achieved in all phases of the educational program.

More Training Needed.—Method in education is therefore largely a matter of *ways of working with individuals and guiding group activity*. It takes a wide variety of forms. Many talents and skills are called for. Some of us will be more gifted and experienced in some phases of leadership than in others. Somewhere in the program will be a place for all we have to offer. Each of us will desire to develop insights and abilities beyond what we now possess. Those who attempt to give leadership in the educational work of the church will sense the great opportunity as well as the responsibility of becoming ever more skilled in the most fruitful ways of guiding growth. The splendid books now available and the helpful courses provided should be given consideration by all who attempt to become "workmen who need not be ashamed."

CHAPTER IV

ORGANIZING FOR CHRISTIAN EDUCATION

If people are to live and work together continuously in a group some form of organization is necessary. The early Christians found this to be the case and the Book of Acts tells the story of the formation of the Mother Church in Jerusalem. Religion has always tended to express itself in some institutional form. Protestantism has found expression in a wide variety of denominations, each with its own plan of organization. Some are highly organized; others operate very simply.

The Importance of Organization.—Instead of being incidental to the life of the local church, the matter of organization may be most significant for the outcomes of its life and work. Organization determines human relationships. It serves as a means of enlisting and using persons. Through it collective thinking and action take place. It makes provision for the gathering together of resources otherwise impossible. Through it responsibility is assigned. Stability and continuity of group life are assured. Principles and procedures in setting up church organization are therefore quite necessary in securing the effective operation of a local parish.

In considering the organization for religious education we must deal with the plans for the *total* church. One of the functions of the church previously mentioned is that of "maintaining a strong effective organization." The church must operate as a whole. There can be no justification for the existence of any organization connected with the church except as it aids in developing Christian persons, in building up the Christian fellowship, and in assisting that fellowship in its outreach into the community and the larger world.

Is Your Church Well Organized?—A group of ministers and church workers were discussing in a seminar the question: how effective is our present church organization? Some of the comments were as follows: "Our church is over-organized." "I am compelled to belong to entirely too many groups." "In our church several organizations are working in the same field." "There is no all-inclusive program-building board or committee." "All the positions in our church are held by a few people." And so the comments ran. Do they sound familiar? These frank criticisms from the "inside" suggest several major difficulties that doubtless characterize many local churches. No one person or group is responsible for these conditions. They have come about through years of unguided development. But each of us is responsible for seeing that they do not continue to exist. In recent years denominational boards of education have made great progress in plans for simpler and more effective local church organization.

Some Guiding Principles.—Most of the efforts at reorganization have been guided by basic principles that have emerged out of past experience and present thinking. The following statements should be carefully considered by local groups in trying to improve their own situation. First, *an organization does not exist for its own sake but as a means to an end*. Whenever an organization gets in the way of effective church work, loses sight of human values and group welfare, it is time to revise or eliminate it. An agency exists solely to aid in realizing some particular goal. Second, *the plan of organization for the church should serve to preserve and promote the unity of the entire constituency*. No group within the church is more important than the church as a whole. The plan of relationships and activities should be such as to develop within all members a dominant loyalty to the parent church and bring all lesser groups into vital relationship to each other and to the church proper.

Third, *the most representative and authoritative body in the entire church should be made responsible for planning the program.* Programs of an age group and for special functions are often planned in a piecemeal fashion. The situation in most churches can be improved only as there comes to exist in the local church a representative body of people charged with the responsibility of integrating the activity of all groups into *one church program.*

Fourth, *the organization should provide opportunity for promoting the fellowship and work of smaller groups within the church and at the same time relating them properly to the parent body.* Smaller groups of people will naturally be formed, such as interest groups, classes, age group fellowships, and service clubs. Many of the richest and most developmental experiences people have will be in these smaller groups. They should be made effective and their activities related to the larger church. Fifth, *the organization should be so planned that it secures the fullest participation possible on the part of all the members of the church.* In developing the spiritual life of individuals as well as effectiveness in church work, there is no substitute for the active participation of all individuals in the church. Organization may hinder or aid in this process.

How Shall the Church Be Organized for Education?— Most of the denominations are providing for the organization of their educational programs along the lines suggested by these principles. We shall indicate here briefly how these principles will be incorporated in a plan of organization. We would need only to substitute a few terms to bring the plan

47

of organization into conformity with that of any one denomination.

One Responsible Planning Body.—Ordinarily the most authoritative body in the local church, such as a Quarterly Conference, Church Session, Council, or in some cases the congregation itself, will create a Church Board or Committee on Education which will be charged with the responsibility of developing and maintaining the educational program of the church. This board or committee should be representative of the entire constituency of the church. Usually it will be composed of the pastor, the church school superintendent, the age group division superintendents if there are such, representatives of such groups as the women's organizations, youth fellowships, missionary agencies, representatives of parents and several members chosen at large because of their interest and fitness in educational work. Such a board or committee should embrace in its membership representatives of all organizations and age groups which function in the educational work of the church. The group should not be too large to meet frequently and operate effectively. Ordinarily its membership will range from nine to twenty-four. Such a group will be capable of *planning a comprehensive and unified educational program.* It should provide for worship, fellowship, study and service, including social, recreational, evangelistic, and missionary activity, and education in the Christian way of life. It should have interlocking membership with other all-church committees, such as finance, missions, and similar committees.

Provision should be made for various small groups associations and activities. These will include departments, classes, clubs, societies, and committees. But they should all be unified and supervised through the Church Board of Education. Many organizations in the local church have developed independently of any overhead supervision, such as a Ladies

48

Aid Society. Others are promoted by and feel responsibility to national boards, such as missionary organizations and young people's societies. In some cases it will take time and tactful leadership to bring these groups into harmonious relations with a Church Board of Education. Unless they are assured they will be given adequate representation and voice in decisions affecting their welfare they will hesitate to relinquish the independence they have enjoyed through the years.

Duties of the Church Board of Education.—In order to understand the working of this Board it will be necessary to get clearly in mind its specific responsibilities. They will include the following:[1]

1. "To make provision for the organization, guidance and supervision of the three Divisions of the church, as follows: the children's division (one to eleven years, inclusive); the youth division (twelve to twenty-three years, inclusive); and the adult division (twenty-four and over). . . ."

2. "To develop a program of Christian education which shall include worship, fellowship, study, and service, use of literature . . . missionary education . . . and other activity. . . ."

3. "To provide for budgeting and expending funds raised throughout the church school."

4. "To plan a program of leadership education for the improvement of workers in service, and for the discovery, selection, and training of prospective workers and leaders."

5. "To provide opportunities for parents and young people to have studies in marriage and Christian homemaking."

6. "To plan the observance of . . . special days."

7. "To observe the fourth Sunday in each month as World Service Sunday. . . ."

8. "To insure that records are accurately kept by the officials of the church school. . . ."

9. "To see that information concerning the work of . . . schools, colleges, universities, and specified student work . . . is given regularly in the church. . . ."

10. "To hold regular meetings (presumably monthly) for the purpose of receiving and passing upon reports and recommen-

dations and for the study of the educational work of the church; and in advance of the opening of the church school year, on recommendation of the general superintendent in concurrence with the pastor, to elect all officers and teachers of the church school. . . ."

11. "To fill all vacancies during the year. . . ."

12. To the list set forth above might well be added the responsibility to represent the church in all forms of inter-church and community educational activities, such as vacation schools, weekday classes, teacher training programs and youth councils.

Provision for Program-building.—It will be readily seen that the chief duties of such a Church Board of Education lie in the field of program-building and supervision. This is the group which will study the needs of the local situation, consider the resources available with which to meet these needs, and plan the program by which to deal with them. They will determine the nature of the grading or grouping possible and desirable. They will wrestle with the problems of supplying officers, teachers, and other leaders for the program. Finance will come under their consideration. But their major responsibility is as suggested above, "to develop a program of Christian education." This task can become a truly creative and inspiring experience for such a group as many a Board is finding it to be. Much depends upon their vision, interest, determination and resourcefulness. In doing this they will of course seek to relate their work closely with that of other groups that may be working within the church, such as the missionary agencies, women's organizations, and finance committees. The pastor and general superintendent are the executive officers responsible for seeing that the policies and plans of the Board are carried out. (Their duties are discussed later.)

Provision is also made for other groups to share in this creative process. There should be in each church a council of children's workers and a council of adult workers and a church council of youth. These councils are designed to bring together the superintendents and leaders of the various departments and other agencies dealing with the respective age groups. Each council should meet monthly or as often as necessary and exercise such supervision over the various programs being promoted within the church for its respective age groups as will avoid duplications and omissions and contribute to the total religious needs of the age group concerned. It is within these councils that much of the detailed planning of the program of Christian education may occur. They are close to the members of the group served. They are usually few in number and can meet with greater frequency. They are in a splendid position to make detailed reports and recommendations to the Church Board of Education for adoption and to the General Workers' Conference for information. Here again is an opportunity for creative and significant planning. Very often these groups function effectively where it seems difficult if not impossible to bring the Church Board of Christian Education or the Workers' Conference into active leadership in the local church.

Democracy at Work in the Local Church.—One of the principles suggested above called for the fullest possible participation of the people of the constituency in the work of the church. Increasing opportunity for participation is provided in such an organization as that under consideration. In addition to the rather large number of people embraced in the membership of the Church Board of Education, and the additional leaders who will participate in the age group councils, provision may well be made for a general Workers' Conference, in each church, composed of the pastor, the general superintendent, the assistant superintendents, other general officers of the church school, and all adult officers and teachers and student officers of the departments of the youth division. The general superintendent or the minister should be the presiding officer of the Workers' Conference. It should meet at least quarterly, while in many churches such a group will hold regular monthly meetings. The Workers' Conference should provide for study and discussion of the educational task of the Church, and for making such recommendations to the Church Board of Education as it may deem advisable. *Here is democracy at work in the local church;* participation, common study, representation, voting power, recommendations, determination of responsibility. Nothing can more fully guarantee the effective operation of a local church program than the full practice of democratic and creative procedure. Surely these are provided for in the plans just set forth. Here many individuals will find opportunity to participate in a variety of ways.

Age Group Organizations.—Emphasis has been placed throughout this book upon the unity of the church's program and organization. However, this need not prevent the members of an age group from creating a strong fellowship and program among themselves. In fact, every effort should be made to encourage such groups in the local church as high school students or young adults to form such an organization as will provide opportunity for their interests, needs and leadership to find full expression. Most denominations are recommending a single agency in the local church through which all the activities of a given age group, such as the Senior Hi youth fellowship, may be planned, including Sunday morning and evening and various through-the-week programs. Committees or commissions are created which act for the entire group in such areas as missions, worship, and recreation. In similar manner young adults are increasingly forming organizations for fellowship, study and service. Each of these groups will operate under the general supervision of the church board or committee on education which will seek to correlate such programs and organizations to those of the church as a whole. In turn each group should be represented on the church's educational committee or board. Specific plans for such age groups are available in the literature of the various denominations.[2] The accompanying chart will serve to illustrate the type of organization suggested here. Such a plan will vary slightly with each denomination, but in general such a blueprint of organization is being recommended by educational authorities.

The Small Church.—But in many instances, it will be felt that these plans are too elaborate for churches with limited membership and resources. This may be entirely true. Provision should be made in any plan of organization for combining and simplifying various groups and relationships. For instance, the Church Board of Education and the Workers' Conference may be combined and perform all the duties normally assigned to each. Even so, it is well to have a small committee from the combined group that may meet frequently and care for matters that need not await meetings of the larger group. Instead of a department for Beginners and another for Primary children one class for each age may be all that can be provided, and divisions for the three age groups utterly unnecessary. Adaptations will need to be worked out in various kinds and sizes of churches.

The program of Christian education which is being proposed here is much broader than that usually referred to as the traditional Sunday school. Every phase of a broad, rich church program involves educational method. Our concern is to understand how the various elements of this program may be most effectively administered. It will not be possible to bring such a conception of the church's educational program into immediate realization. It will require time for agencies to be modified, for people to be educated to different ideas, and for details of its smooth operation to be worked out. But it is most gratifying to have a blueprint that points in the

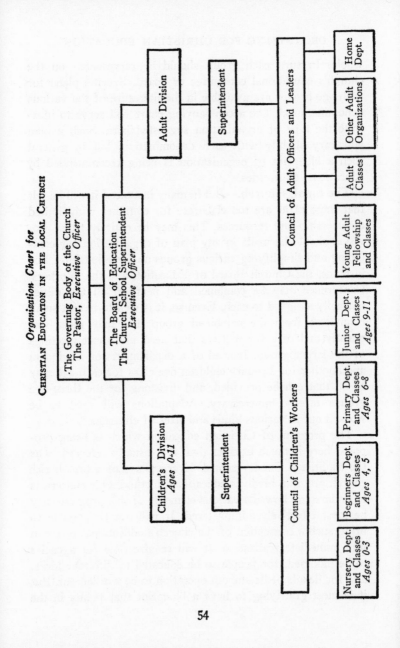

Organization Chart for
CHRISTIAN EDUCATION IN THE LOCAL CHURCH

The Governing Body of the Church
The Pastor, *Executive Officer*

The Board of Education
The Church School Superintendent
Executive Officer

Children's Division
Ages 0-11

Superintendent

Council of Children's Workers

| Nursery Dept. and Classes *Ages 0-3* | Beginners Dept. and Classes *Ages 4, 5* | Primary Dept. and Classes *Ages 6-8* | Junior Dept. and Classes *Ages 9-11* |

Adult Division

Superintendent

Council of Adult Officers and Leaders

| Young Adult Fellowship and Classes | Adult Classes | Other Adult Organizations | Home Dept. |

54

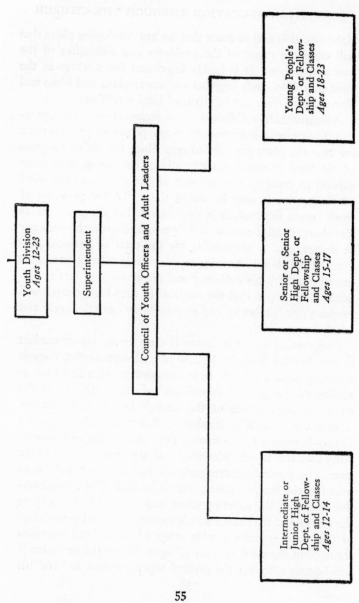

Youth Division
Ages 12-23

Superintendent

Council of Youth Officers and Adult Leaders

Young People's Dept. or Fellowship and Classes
Ages 18-23

Senior or Senior High Dept. or Fellowship and Classes
Ages 15-17

Intermediate or Junior High Dept. of Fellowship and Classes
Ages 12-14

55

right direction and to know that we are developing plans that will eliminate many of the problems and difficulties of the past and present. It is highly important for workers in the local church to study together the newer plans and ideas and then to work them out in terms of local conditions.

Administrative Officers.—No organization is self-operative. It requires administrators. Some person or persons must see that the plans are carried out. Since the entire program of the local church is an educational enterprise, it is quite natural to consider the minister of the church as the chief administrator. It may be stated thus: "In the program of work herein outlined, it is understood that the pastor is as elsewhere, in all the work of the pastoral charge, the preacher in charge, and is responsible for the total educational program of the church. Nothing in this plan is to be construed as interfering with his authority and responsibility." [3] It is certainly to be hoped that the minister in each local church will exercise this "authority and responsibility" as effectively and wisely as possible.

Cooperating with the pastor is the general superintendent of the church school. In the new plan of organization there is naturally some confusion as to the exact position and responsibility of the general superintendent. In reality he is the chief executive officer of the Church Board of Education. This is a responsibility he shares, of course, with the pastor. It may become a much broader and more inclusive responsibility than that usually identified with the church school of the past. The general superintendent's responsibility will be as broad as the Board's conception of its task. The administrative duties of the superintendent may be confined simply to the sessions of the church school meeting on Sunday morning, or they may embrace a wide range of educational activities throughout the week and for all ages. Under the new plan it will be necessary for the general superintendent to "feel his way" into the newer responsibilities. In many larger churches these broader relationships and duties will be assigned to a professionally trained director of religious education or associate minister. It is important for the Board, the minister, and the superintendent to think through carefully the exact duties of the superintendent. His work should become increasingly supervisory, that is, be concerned with measures by which the total program may be *improved* in its effectiveness.

In the larger churches the divisional or departmental superintendents will assume considerable responsibility for administering the program in their respective age groups. It is highly desirable that they shall feel the full responsibility for the quality of the work of their departments and yet respond to the plans and suggestions of the Church Board of Education. It will be the duty of the general superintendent and pastor to interpret to these associate officers the objective and plans of the Board. An effective administrator will build up about the common task a group of loyal, cooperative staff members who together with him will strive to realize the objectives of the program.

In the last analysis, any organization exists solely to "get things done." If it seems impossible or undesirable to try to form a Church Board of Education, let the pastor or the superintendent, or both together, work with whatever group of teachers, officers, parents and other individuals are available to outline and supervise such a program as they can develop. A few people seriously studying and faithfully working at a local situation can bring about truly worthwhile improvements. Surely in any local church such a group at least might be enlisted in the work normally handled by a Church Board of Education. What is absolutely necessary is that at least *some one person* have a vision and willingness to do something about it, and try to enlist others in working toward the realization of the vision.

57

CHAPTER V

THE CHURCH A CHRISTIAN FELLOWSHIP

Fellowship among Christians has been an important aspect of the religion of Jesus since the time he gathered about himself the chosen twelve. The new religion depended mainly for its spread upon the inspiration and training that came from intimate association with Jesus for three short years on the part of these ordinary men. Through the early years the Christian community found close fellowship absolutely necessary as the few scattered groups of disciples were surrounded by an indifferent and hostile society. They needed mutual encouragement, protection and help. Sometimes they met in the home of one of their number; frequently they gathered in the Jewish synagogue; at times they came together in an abandoned quarry; eventually they built meeting places of their own. But they always sought fellowship.

Whenever Christianity has been true to its genius it has fostered close and rich association among its members. "Blest be the tie that binds our hearts in Christian love." This love has been the saving and sustaining factor in the lives of countless numbers of Christians. Throughout the centuries Christianity's appeal to those outside the church has been in part the attraction of fellowship with people who were attempting *together* to follow the lowly Nazarene. It has helped to make converts. Such fellowship has been a chief means of holding the new convert to his decision and training him in the Christian way of life.

58

The Significance of Fellowship.—Group association ministers to basic human needs. Each of us desires friends. We instinctively crave human comradeship. We desire intensely to feel that we "belong," that we are wanted by those we like to be with. We hunger for recognition. Modern psychology and psychiatry are enabling us to appreciate ever more fully what we have always known, namely, how important these human associations are in the development of wholesome personality and in promoting group life. Just as truly they are revealing to what extent the failure to secure these social experiences is the direct cause of the most common personality difficulties and problems of social adjustment.

Life is largely a matter of social contacts and relationships. The individual who makes and sustains these contacts naturally and easily, who knows how properly to relate himself to the group, who possesses skill in association and leadership among others, has acquired social grace and ability that constitute some of the most coveted means of enjoying life. Recent statements of the objectives of education and character development include strong emphases on social attitudes and skills. Likewise, the more recent statements of the purposes of Christian education include emphasis upon social relations. It will be recalled that among the functions of the church outlined in Chapter One is this one: "To provide fellowship through every means possible and for all ages."

People will seek such fellowship in one way or another. If they cannot find friendship and enjoyable association in a clean wholesome environment they will seek it elsewhere. There can be no doubt that the popularity of the pool room, the tavern, the street corner, the club or the road house, arises from the fact that those who frequent them, whether the gangster, the juvenile delinquent, the habitual boozer, gay youth out for a "good time" or the respectable citizen seeking relaxation, find there a form of fellowship and a sense of being welcome. The church is in no position to criticize many of these places unless she is making adequate and attractive provision for what these people want. Furthermore, she will do well to capitalize on these instinctive desires and needs not only to minister to them but also to cause them to serve the higher ends of religious living.

The Uniqueness of Christian Fellowship.—Christian fellowship is the highest and finest form of human association. It embraces all that has just been noted plus that unique quality known as *Christian love*. If the God of Jesus Christ may be regarded as *positive outgoing love and goodwill,* a goodwill that constantly seeks the wellbeing of all people, then those who meet in the name of this God are attempting to realize and release in their midst the mightiest known force for human redemption. The congregation of Christians is frequently referred to as "the beloved community." It is a concrete expression of "the family of God." It ought to be a living demonstration before others of what people are like when they are filled with the spirit of Jesus Christ. One of the major efforts of Jesus was to teach people how to get along with one another. Whenever he was successful, of Christians it was said, "Behold how these Christians love one another." His most exacting teachings and most inspiring utterances dealt with human relations. "Love the Lord thy God . . . *and thy neighbor as thyself."* Who is "thy neighbor"? One of the choicest stories of all literature answers that question for all time.

Jesus demonstrated by his life, teachings and death that "greater love hath no man than this that a man lay down his life for his friend." This represents the loftiest interpretation of human fellowship that has ever been conceived. It has its inspiration in the belief that such love is rooted in the nature of God, that it is part of the moral structure of the universe. "God so loved the world that he gave his only be-gotten son that whosoever believeth in him should not perish but have everlasting life." No group of people on earth stand committed to such an exalted and demanding conception of human relations as those who profess to be Christians, who are attempting to fulfill in their midst and spread throughout the world the true spirit of Christian love.

It is therefore impossible to conceive of the Christian religion without fellowship. *The Christian religion is a fellowship.* In a real sense *there is no salvation outside the church,* apart from the believing, fellowshiping congregation. The "family of God" is the most inclusive, dynamic idea of divine-human relations we can think of, the Fatherhood of God and the brotherhood of man.

Types of Fellowship in the Church.—When one begins seriously to look for fellowship in the local church he finds a great variety of opportunities for its expression. Practically all forms of church life and work, or of Christian education, may provide fellowship that is life-enriching. These oppor-tunities are found in the church school class, the Boy Scout troop meeting, the youth fellowship, the missionary study group, the prayer meeting, the activities of the women's or-ganization, the worship service on Sunday morning, as well as in the sessions of the church board of education, the workers' conference, the official board, the mothers' circle and the party of the Primary children. In fact, the full list-ing of these opportunities would bring into review practically all forms of group life and activity in the local church.

What opportunities for vital Christian fellowship are offered in the average local church! They include the small and the large group, the infrequent informal committee meet-ing and the regularly recurring formal worship service of the church. Our concern should not necessarily be to increase the number and frequency of such meetings, but rather to make sure that each of them yields helpful, enjoyable association. The teacher who can develop happy, helpful fellowship in his class in their Sunday meetings and in the through-the-week contacts, the youth counselor who can make the youth fellowship meeting on Sunday evening and at other times an inviting social experience, the men's or women's group that in addition to other aspects of its work creates a warm friendly atmosphere, is adding something of vital significance to the on-going program. *At least some such experiences must be made available to each and every member of the church constituency.*

Such fellowship as we have been considering does not just automatically occur in these groups. Committee meetings, church services, class sessions, and even parties may easily be devoid of the very thing they are meant to provide, namely, wholesome human association. In all too many cases people *do not* feel at home, they *do not* feel that they "belong," they have *no* sense of responsibility in the undertakings of the group, they feel *no* rapport with the leader. We must become keenly aware of the conditions that prevent the realization of friendship and fellowship and also know by what means such fellowship may most surely be created.

Barriers to Christian Fellowship.—There are many conditions that prevent the realization of wholesome Christian fellowship. Jesus encountered many of them. Paul provides a catalogue of them in his letters to the early Christians. At least some of them are familiar to most of us. It is one thing to be able to discover what is wrong with a given situation. It is a more difficult task to correct it. It may help us to have some of them clearly in mind as we discuss the problem. (1) Certainly we need to note first, the failure of many Christians to appreciate the real meaning and experience of fellowship. They often fail to understand and enter into this fellowship on the distinctly Christian level. Hence they have nothing to share; they do not miss it when it is lacking in various social groupings. They are not concerned about providing it more abundantly in the local church. It is only as we become aware of both its meaning and of its significance in individual and social life that we seek definitely to realize it in its fullness. Such a lack of appreciation thus prevents the development of full fellowship throughout the church.

(2) Then there are the attitudes that characterize all too many of us, and that prevent fellowship: attitudes of jealousy, distrust, hatred, envy, suspicion, fear. We are disposed to be exclusive in our relations, to form cliques, to associate only with those we like. Many people are naturally shy and reticent, find it difficult to take the initiative in forming friendships. Others are mastered by fears, fear of not being accepted or liked, fear of being shunned or disregarded. Some feel insecure or inadequate in dealing with others and hence are inclined to keep to themselves. Many take offense at the slightest provocation of seeming neglect, indifference, or imagined wrong. How common these attitudes are among us, all of us realize. We also know that they interfere greatly with the achievement of group fellowship and wholesome personal relations.

There is no easy and sure way of eliminating these unfortunate attitudes, as those of us who have struggled against them in our own experience know all too well. Modern psychology is providing great help in dealing with these attitudes. The teachings of the Bible, especially the New Testament, deal extensively with them. The surest remedy for all of them is the spirit of Jesus Christ, sincere outgoing love and good will toward all, including "your enemies and those that *despitefully* use you." We need to remind ourselves again and again that "perfect love casteth out fear." Forgetfulness of self, centering our thought and affections upon others, being "kindly affectioned one toward another," represent the best advice that the New Testament can offer.

It is the continuing testimony of countless numbers of Christians that these undesirable attitudes and feelings can be conquered, that love can supplant hate, that freedom, self-confidence and social ease can take the place of insecurity and undue self-consciousness; that envy and jealousy can give way to joy and pride in the success and achievements of others. Such is the power of Christian love if given half a chance in our lives. A heavy responsibility rests upon the Christian community to demonstrate daily in a world full of strife, evil, ill will, and hatred the healing and saving power of the "beloved community." This means of course that the fellowship we are discussing must by all means increasingly characterize the total body of Christians, crossing denominational lines, leaping readily over racial and social barriers, freely bringing together in fellowship those of different economic and cultural backgrounds. In such a Christian fellowship alone lies the hope of universal peace and world brotherhood.

Conditions Not Favorable for Fellowship.—(3) Failure to achieve fellowship in the local church may also often grow out of a failure to create the necessary conditions. Such conditions include setting up occasions for bringing people together frequently enough to form close social bonds and easy familiarity, providing them with the kind of activities that promote acquaintanceship and growing comradeship, discovering common interests, learning how to bring together those who would not naturally and spontaneously join in social activity. Often the church offers an exceedingly narrow and limited range of social and recreational activities and consequently fails to enlist the cooperation and response of large sections of its constituency.

(4) Failure to provide fellowship often grows out of a

64

lack of leadership in the local situation. The provision of many of these forms of activity does not involve highly trained leaders. But it is essential that people be found or trained who can promote sociability, lead in games, direct groups in song and play, and who know how to uncover and use talents and resources represented in the average group.

Ways of Promoting Fellowship.—There is no sure formula that will guarantee Christian fellowship. We will need to be alive to those simple ways that experience has taught us aid individuals and groups in their social development. Some of the more important ways have already been indicated. Others may be suggested. In fact, one of the best ways of going about this matter in a local church is for the board of education or some comparable group to undertake a thorough study of the situation in their church and canvass the ways of making Christian fellowship more meaningful to the total constituency. Each age group council or committee will surely want to do this. Such participation in studying, planning and carrying forward activity is in itself one of the essential means of promoting the very thing we are concerned for.

Three basic steps will be readily appreciated: *first,* people must get acquainted; *second,* they must come to feel that they belong to a great fellowship, and *third,* they need to enjoy and participate in the life of the church. Failure at any one of these points will mean failure in the objectives we have in mind. First, therefore, it is essential that people meet one another, that they discover friends. A church school class where each member feels he knows all other members *by name,* that week by week cultivates friendliness, that follows up its absentee members, that holds special recreational, social and service sessions, that cements in devotional exercises the ordinary bonds of friendship with "special reference to the Great Friend," is well on the way to making the most of friendship and fellowship.

The committee or board that holds its meeting in a comfortable, informal physical setting, that cultivates the spirit of good cheer, that takes time for happy social amenities, that keeps the discussion free from bickering, quarrelling, and discourtesies, that recognizes the contributions, talents and needs of each member is very likely to experience genuine Christian fellowship.

The church that plans for fairly frequent gatherings of the total constituency, that has an occasional picnic, frequent church night gatherings, will find itself entering into an ever more meaningful experience of fellowship. Such gatherings should often bring the entire constituency, young and old, together. Most churches need more of such a happy intermingling of ages. Our modern graded program of Christian education has made remarkable contributions, but many are feeling that it has segregated the various ages too sharply and fails to provide sufficient total church fellowship. We are discovering that there are many interests and activities that young and old alike may share and enjoy. Let the primary or beginner children entertain their parents in *their own room* and in *their own way* some Saturday or Sunday afternoon. Where such has been done the most frequent comment on the part of both children and parents is, "When can we do this again?" Or let the Junior Hi's plan an evening of sharing with their parents, possibly an evening fellowship dinner or a late Sunday afternoon lap lunch at which time they can sing and play together, report on projects or work accomplished, share in pupil-led worship, and listen to comments and "advice" from oldsters and youngsters. Such gatherings pay rich dividends in comradeship, and better understanding and cooperation. One of the major objectives of church work with young children is to make them feel at home in the church, to find friends and to enjoy association with their leaders.

Fellowship on Sunday Morning and After.—The church that carefully and consistently cultivates a warm welcome and a friendly spirit with its regular church service will find itself increasing its ministry to its own members and drawing outsiders to its services. Frequently ministers and others have a limited appreciation of the fellowship possibilities of this greatest gathering of the week in most churches. Not only that, but in some cases greetings, fraternizing, and lingering for conversation after church has been frowned upon. Quite the reverse should be the case. People who may not have seen each other for a week or more, or who have just become acquainted, should be encouraged to tarry after the service to get better acquainted and to lay the foundation for further social contacts. A few churches provide a Sunday dinner after church primarily to promote acquaintanceship. In some cases it facilitates the meetings of committees and other groups that find it difficult to get together during the week.

There is no substitute for the friendships that grow out of calling. Visitation need not be confined to the usual pastoral calling. In fact, the more recent trend has been the enlistment of many lay persons in visiting. Calls are made not only upon the constituency for better acquaintanceship but also for the discovery and enlistment of people not now identified with the local church. When carefully planned, carried out in the right spirit, and properly followed up, genuine evangelism occurs. Friendly interest and personal acquaintanceship are first steps in evangelism. Those who take part in such work often report a new appreciation of the church, a deeper enthusiam for its ministries to the people in the community, and a revitalization of their own religious experience. Many a teacher or club leader has greatly enriched the fellowship of his group and gained rapport with individual members by visiting them in their homes.

Fellowship in Questing and Serving.—A form of fellowship which some people crave is that provided by intimate association with others in projects of sacrificial service, or in the quest for truth, or in "the practice of the presence of God" through some form of group devotional activity. For many these forms of activity will provide the finest and most profitable experiences of fellowship. Here they feel their keenest sense of comradeship and find their greatest satisfaction in shared activity. There will be found in many churches, there might well be cultivated in all churches, small groups of people studying social issues and engaging in some form of social pioneering, or questing together in a "cell" for a more vivid awareness of God's presence in their lives, or seeking together to get a more intelligent and satisfying faith. So long as these forms of association are kept wholesome and do not become exclusive they are certainly to be encouraged. They may well resemble in a small way that group of twelve disciples who shared intimately with the Nazarene in his walks, his teachings, his dealings with people, the meals in the upper room and possibly his long vigils with his Heavenly Father.

The Role of Recreation.—There is a growing recognition within and without the church of the part recreation may play in promoting fellowship and in contributing to wholesome personality development and group life. This is especially true as modern life becomes more complex, hurried, and artificial. Among the healing forces that may be utilized is that of play, indoor and outdoor activities, the cultivation of hobbies, the acquiring of skills that bring rich satisfactions in personal enjoyment and that enhance social relations. Such books as Overstreet's *A Guide to Civilized Leisure* and Jack's *Recreation* present a philosophy of play that is to be taken seriously if modern people are to ward off diseases of mind and body and learn how to counteract the maddening tempo of present-day life. People by the thousands are learning all over again how to play, to sing, and to create. They are discovering the deeper satisfactions that are to be found, not in the vogue of sitting in theaters and bleachers to be entertained by others, but rather by participating in a wide range of recreation. Summer camps, city parks, playgrounds and forest preserves are springing up all over the country offering more and more people, young and old, the opportunity to enjoy nature and to recover some of the naturalness and simplicity of living.

The church should not be a laggard or constitute a hindrance in providing such forms of activity. Indeed, the church has long been a leader in providing camps and similar programs for her youth. There is now every indication that interest and activity in this field will increase rather than decrease. For church leaders appreciate the dynamic learning and growing experiences such forms of education and living provide. Church leaders are also learning that certain forms of recreation can do more to bridge barriers, break down undesirable inhibitions and attitudes, help people find release from unnatural and artificial restraints and to discover how to throw themselves wholeheartedly into group activities than almost any other thing.

Children and youth should come early to understand that they do not need to go to questionable places or engage in undesirable forms of recreations. The church should demonstrate to them its desire to provide play and recreation that is both attractive and wholesome. Undoubtedly there will be an increase in cooperation among churches and other agencies of the community committed to high ideals in recreation. Across the country there have been many instances of splendid cooperation and youth have immeasurably benfited from them.

It will be readily seen why "fellowship" is so central in the life and work of the church, why it has been increasingly emphasized as a major element in the curriculum of Christian education. It will be recalled that among the functions of the church are these two: "To provide fellowship for all ages in the church," and "to extend the fellowship to others through evangelism, recruitment and missions and other means." There has not always been the vision and concern over fellowship as has come about in recent years. Hence it is that in connection with studying the scriptures, joining in worship services, engaging in projects of social service, one finds as a most important part of church activity the creation and enjoyment of Christian fellowship, whether that fellowship grows out of a personal counseling relationship, sharing worship together, a pupil-teacher-comradeship, or comes from some form of joyous recreation.

CHAPTER VI

BRINGING OTHERS INTO THE FELLOWSHIP

If Christian fellowship is all that has been claimed for it, if Christians find that it means so much to them, then surely they should be eager to share this fellowship with others. This eagerness to bring others to enjoy its blessings has been one of the unique aspects of Christianity down through the centuries. Christianity has ever been an *evangelistic* religion; it has always been marked by *missionary zeal*. Beginning with Jesus and the twelve disciples, soon the new religion had converts throughout Palestine. The missionary zeal of the new religion found its greatest embodiment in the new convert Paul. He carried the Good News throughout Asia Minor, into Greece, and thence to Rome. He became the inspiration for subsequent centuries.

The Great Commission.—The Disciples had a great commission. They believed that God had revealed himself in a unique manner in their crucified and risen Lord. He was the Good News of Salvation. He was ultimately to bring into captivity unto himself all races and nations of mankind. They believed that Jesus himself had given the commission, "Go ye therefore, and make disciples of all nations, baptizing them into the name of the Father, and of the Son, and of the Holy Spirit, teaching them to observe all things whatsoever I have commanded you; and lo, I am with you always, even unto the end of the world." [1] That commission has rested heavily upon all branches and all generations of Christians.

71

It is as fresh and compelling today as when first uttered. "The evangelization of the world in our generation" has been the conscious or unconscious purpose of generation after generation of believing Christians, never more so than today.

A new urgency in Christian missions is upon us. There is tragic need throughout the world. A staggering task of reclamation confronts Christians, especially those in America who have been only lightly touched by the ravages of war. This urgency should arouse Christians everywhere to increase many fold their missionary and service efforts. The healing, reviving, and inspiring power of Christianity must be brought to bear upon the lives of countless numbers of people. No institution can do this but the church. The church cannot render this ministry to needy people without the active, intelligent, and continuous cooperation of those who constitute it.

This all-embracing outreach of the Christian religion is born of the spirit and teachings of Jesus who would not be walled in by the narrow prejudices and limited outlook of his religious contemporaries, who disregarded all barriers of class, race and condition of life, who was convinced that what he came to give was for everybody, all men, everywhere. His was a universal salvation. The *missionary* and *evangelistic outreach* is native to Christianity. One cannot be a real Christian without at the same time sharing in this positive concern for all people everywhere. Thus the effort *to extend the fellowship becomes a major function of the modern church.* It is central in the program of Christian education. It is an integral part of Christian living.

The Outreach Abroad.—Traditionally, the evangelistic work of Protestant churches has taken a two-fold direction, missions at home and missions abroad, distinguishing the geographical areas in which the missionary spirit found expression. In the "home" field we have usually thought in terms of recruitment, evangelism, social reconstruction, Christian nurture. Abroad, the idea of "missions" has prevailed and has come to have a broad interpretation, evangelism, education, social service, medical care and even agricultural training. "Home" and "foreign" outreaches are now regarded as one continuing task of the church. For modern Christians to remain ignorant of and indifferent to this phase of the church's program, for youth to grow up in the church without catching the world-wide vision, being stirred by the wide-open opportunity, being challenged by the great unfinished task, would be tragic. Especially is this true in the light of recent events. The last world war has made all men aware of the nearness and accessibility of peoples and cultures which previously were remote and unknown to most of them. The travels of military men have made not only these men, but also the families and friends to whom they have written, aware that Christian missionaries had decades ago sought out backward and needy people and attempted to bring them some of the blessings of democracy and Christianity. "They found the church there" has become one of the most significant commentaries on the missionary outreach of the modern church.

For centuries the Christian church has alone carried the burden of this world outreach. It alone attempted to seek out backward people, to spread education, medicine, sanitation, to secure the release of women from conditions worse than slavery, and to carry the Bible and Christian education to countless numbers of people who did not have them. Other agencies now make some of these contributions. Yet the recent world war has revealed afresh to thousands of military men and others, the continuing unselfish and heroic work of Christian missionaries throughout the world. Surely the church has been "on the march"!

Frontiers at Home.—In like manner, but perhaps in a less spectacular way, the church has steadily reached out across the plains, valleys, mountains, and deserts of our country. It accompanied the pioneers who were forever pushing back the frontiers of civilization. Wherever people went the church went with them and sought to minister to their spiritual needs in the new community. Today most of the typical frontiers have vanished. Instead, we have new types of frontiers. Some are rural, some urban, but they are real and challenging. There are radical movements within cities, residential sections transformed into industrial and manufacturing "belts." Within a decade or so native populations are supplanted by colonies of foreign-born people, or an influx of Negroes from the South transforms a neighborhood overnight. These constitute the "urban frontiers" of today. To minister to these moving populations constitutes an evangelistic outreach that challenges the best leadership of the church.

Or we find other frontiers in the migratory groups that live in tents, trailers, and temporary shacks, as they move from "crop to crop," seeking employment and scanty means of livelihood. In certain sections of the country are large numbers of tenant farmers, "share-croppers" and mountain groups, to whom and to whose children many of the necessities of a rich and abundant life are denied. Such sections of the population of our "America the Beautiful" constitute the pioneer fields for those dominated by the Christian spirit, who have a positive outgoing good will toward all God's children and who would share with them all that democracy and Christianity may mean in physical, cultural and spiritual well-being. The recent war has caused vast shifts in population giving rise to "trailer cities" and new housing developments that call for new ministries on the part of the churches.

Protestants are challenged today by the large numbers in our population who have escaped or are indifferent to the call to become Christian and enter into the fellowship and service of the church. These millions are living in our midst seemingly uninfluenced by the church. Some twenty-five millions of children and youth are growing up without formal religious instruction. Surely in this great number of unchurched people is to be found a field "white unto the harvest." All the evangelistic zeal, the trained laborers, and continued activity of the Christian church need to be directed into this "vineyard."

Modern Evangelism.—So far as the age-old processes of evangelism are concerned there is nothing particularly new; there is no "sure-fire" formula, no modern panacea for all our problems. Most of the effective ways of winning people to Christ have been known for centuries. It is largely a matter of acting on what we already know. If anything is necessary it is *a fresh realization that people must be brought to a consciousness of their need of God,* that our indifference to these needs must be changed to a concern and passion to share the blessings of Christianity. Our spasmodic and half-hearted efforts must become continuous and disciplined work to bring people into the fellowship of the community of Christians. We have learned to be more systematic, to make actual lists of names of people who ought to be reached, to enlist the services of many church members in missions to their neighbors and to the unknown within their communities, to organize the "seventy" as Jesus did, and send them out in "twos" to press the claims of Christ and the church. We are learning that young people and children can engage in such evangelistic activity, that they are effective in reaching those of their own age. Many ministers are making their membership training program thoroughly evangelistic as well as educational in nature. The older "revival meetings" doubtless have their place in certain situations, but they are being supplanted by month-by-month, year-round evangelism that brings into the church a continuous flow of new recruits. These methods are being stressed with both ministers and lay people in the various denominational "crusades" and interdenominational "teaching missions" of recent years.

Training for Evangelism.—Since evangelism aims to bring these people into vital association within the church fellowship as well as to discipleship to Christ, various groups will naturally become the centers of recruiting efforts. The high school fellowship *may* be one of the most active evangelistic units in the local church as it reaches out to bring youth of the community into its church program. Young people who have just been married and are establishing homes and families have great need of friendship and mutual help with those of their own age. Hence the young adult fellowship *may* and *should* reach out to young adults in the community. A men's Bible class, the women's society, a special visitation group, each and all *may* be the center and motivation of increasing evangelistic activity. Teachers, youth counselors, members of church boards of education, stewards, deacons, and many other leaders should consider themselves special "ambassadors of Christ" in their various contacts with people within and outside the church. Specific training in evangelism should be given these various groups. There is an increasing awareness of the possibilities of using such activities as week day and vacation schools, summer camps and institutes, and adult schools of religion as means of reaching and enlisting growing numbers of the great unchurched masses in our communities. *True evangelism means generating among all Christians something of the sincere, positive, outgoing love and good will toward all people that marked Jesus in all his relations with all people at all times.*

Educating for World Friendship.—Our purpose here is threefold: first, to provide information; second, to develop attitudes, appreciations, and interests; and third, to lead people into appropriate action.

Facts are dynamic; full and accurate information is moving. Let the facts be known about approaching famine in China and people will be moved to action. Let the conditions surrounding share-croppers be accurately described and some people are bound to respond to the need depicted. The first responsibility of those attempting to lead people into activity on behalf of others in need is to "give them the facts." Statistics regarding the number of unchurched in a community, even in the small town where everybody seems to know everybody else, will usually stir church members to some form of evangelism. The knowledge that millions of children and youth are not now being taught religion is one means by which men and money are being enlisted in campaigns to "reach the unchurched." Graphic pictures of conditions affecting the lives of women in sections of India, natives in exploited Liberia, and the backward tribes in Borneo will necessarily precede any effort to arouse people to attempt to minister to such groups. Today American Christians need graphic portrayal of the vast numbers of churches that must be rebuilt in Europe and the East and of local churches that will need aid in re-establishing their work.

The church has greatly improved her literature regarding the unreached and unsaved. Books, magazines, pamphlets, tracts, maps, and pictures are all artfully employed to present information to arouse the evangelistic and missionary zeal of all ages in the church. Much splendid visual material is being made available in the form of film strips, slides and motion picture films.[2] There is little excuse for any church, no matter how far removed from the main highways of the world, not having full and accurate information regarding any and all groups at home and abroad with whom the church is attempting to share the full gospel of Jesus Christ. A penny postcard sent to the missionary boards or boards of education of any of the denominations will bring splendid material to the aid of any teacher, parent or minister.

Groups in Action.—Some Juniors in a certain church were considering whether to attempt to raise some "extra" money for some form of service. A nurse from one of the backward mountain regions of the country was invited to tell of her work in relieving suffering, promoting sanitary ways of living, reducing sickness, and bringing some of the normal benefits of modern life to these people. The Juniors responded enthusiastically to this appeal. Their question was settled. New understanding and appreciation had been developed. Action followed.

A group of children, reflecting the attitudes of their parents, were resentful of the presence of a Japanese boy in their neighborhood. He was one of the many displaced Japanese of World War II. The teacher of the church school led them in a discussion of why the Japanese boy was in their community, how they would feel if they were in his place, and how they would like to be treated. The children were having a new experience. New appreciations and insights were being developed, and these in turn led to totally different attitudes and responses.

During a recent instance of strong racial feeling in a suburban community, adult leaders brought together several white youth who were active in the churches of the community. They were challenged to inform themselves about the issues and incidents that were arousing such strong feeling and to confer with Negro youth attending the same high school. This these young people did, at first with reluctance and misgiving. Their serious study of the problem, their friendly attitude toward their Negro schoolmates, and their frank discussion with them did much to avert a serious outbreak of race feeling in the high school itself. The Negro-White youth group pledged themselves to continued fellowship and joint action whenever it seemed necessary. Social imagination and fellow feeling were awakened in the young people of both races when challenged and given opportunity to look at situations through the eyes of others. They accepted the teaching of Jesus as their guide in attempting to deal with critical issues.

During the recent world-wide shortage of food, a group of young parents secured literature and speakers depicting the shortage of vitamins and vital foods in certain needy countries. They formed a plan for saving and collecting fats, oils, and other most needed materials and sending them direct to groups, particularly children in selected sections of the needy areas. With such material went personal messages interpreting their Christian concern for those in need and inviting them to accept the Christian faith if they had not already done so. Correspondence developed that was a source of great interest and profit to all involved.

Ways of Promoting World Friendship.—Some of the ways of building attitudes and stimulating action have already been suggested. Let us review and add to them. (1) Securing and using literature; (2) bringing resource persons before the group, members of other races, missionaries, people who have lived and traveled among others; (3) have members of other races and social groups represent their own groups; (4) learn the games and hobbies of other people as a means of "seeing life through their eyes"; (5) set up exhibits of curios, costumes, art and other forms of cultural materials of various people; (6) have exchange visits, especially with strange or new groups close by, such as young people from the Swedish colony, the "Italian center," the Negroes across the tracks; (7) use story and biographical material especially with children; (8) canvass and use the growing body of visualized material that is being made available. Many of these activities seem commonplace and undramatic, yet it is through just such relationships and activities that young and old are becoming world-minded. The church that does not develop and carry forward vigorously its share of such projects is failing its own people, a needy world and its own Christ.

The alert growing church, or church school, will attempt in every way to provide a wide range of information along these lines to all age groups. Church school and missionary literature of most denominations provides a rich body of resource material. In some cases the information about needy groups at home and abroad will be graded and highly specialized; at other times such knowledge about "others" will be passed throughout the church, all groups, young and old, sharing in changing attitudes and resulting forms of action. A study of the church's outreach into Africa or South America may be the theme for a quarter running throughout all departments. Training will be given to all leaders of all groups. The minister will deal with this theme from the pulpit and other public meetings. Projects of giving and service will afford all members of families and of the entire constituency opportunity to make concrete contribution. Or following a fresh study of the blessings Christianity is bestowing upon those who are in the church, the entire constituency be enlisted in efforts to reach the unreached in the community seeking to bring them into the fellowship of the church. A careful review of the various lesson systems of the denominations will reveal that a generous number of units dealing with the missionary projects of the church are scattered throughout the various age group offerings. As has been suggested, sometimes these are individualized units, at other times they are part of a church-wide emphasis upon some particular mission field.

Christian Stewardship.—The basis of practically all missionary work, evangelism and social service is the principle of Christian stewardship. Discipleship to Christ means *the stewardship of life*, the dedication of one's abilities, time, energy and money to the work of the Kingdom of God. This is one of the most important elements of Christian living and one that must be made ever more effective in the attitudes and practices of Christians, especially young people. While the giving of money is by no means the sum total of stewardship, it is highly essential in promoting the work of the church. Systematic giving is rapidly supplanting irregular, unplanned contributions. Yearly pledges, weekly envelopes, and carefully kept individual financial accounts are becoming common in churches. Especially is it important that children and young people be given training in systematic giving. A certain church was closed for several summer months for repairs. With the opening Sundays in the fall, bushel baskets were required to care for the envelopes brought by the children and young people who had made pledges and were faithfully fulfilling their obligations of financial stewardship.

It is essential that Christians understand and accept the broader meaning of stewardship. It does not mean that they will all be called upon to give full time service in the church, but it does mean that young and old will be asked to invest a proper proportion of their time, money, energy and abilities in the work of the Kingdom. It does mean that each Christian will regard his whole life as a trust from God to be used not for self alone but for self *and others*. We will find in a later discussion the necessity of securing the services of a large number of people who will be required in leadership in various activities in the church. Their services cannot be secured unless the principle of stewardship is fully accepted in their discipleship. As modern folk find their lives increasingly crowded with activities and multitudes of temptations to become absorbed in things of secondary importance, it will be doubly necessary to challenge them to give themselves generously to the church and the Kingdom.

A Christian Imperative.—What is needed above all things is a continuing constructive program of evangelization and missionary work in each local church. Responsibility for such planning will need to rest with some group or groups. Certainly the Church Board or Committee on Education should make sure that these emphases are being carried out effectively throughout the church. A committee or commission on world friendship may well be established for the entire church, with representatives from all age groups, and given responsibility to promote study and activity along these lines. They should maintain close contact with their denominational boards and world-wide inter-denominational agencies. They should conduct training conferences, create a library of resource materials, set up a book table or literature display at appropriate times, locate resource persons, aid and encourage the minister to deal in sermons with topics and problems in these areas as frequently as seems wise, and relate the total church program of missions and evangelism to such programs in the community and in larger relations.

A certain church, typical of many churches throughout the country, was plodding along in a self-satisfied, self-centered way. A young minister came to serve it, a man with social vision and a broad world outlook. He believed that the main business of the church is to bring others into its fellowship. Before long he had groups among the various ages at work, first informing themselves about the needs of people near at hand and throughout the world, and then undertaking significant evangelistic and missionary projects. Nothing had stirred this church so much in years. It experienced new life; it sensed a mission; it rejoiced in new accomplishments. It had begun itself to fulfill the great commission of our Lord.

CHAPTER VII

WORSHIP IN THE CHURCH

People need God in their lives. Today people seem desperately eager for something that satisfies their inner hunger, some cause to give themselves to wholeheartedly, someone to whom to look with hope for the future. Modern man is in a desperate plight and he is beginning to realize it. He needs guidance, moral courage, spiritual strength, and the willingness to sacrifice for what he knows is right. Where shall he get these things? The source of such help is to be found in the Christian religion, especially in the personal devotions and group worship which it provides.

The Need of Worship.—We all need the consciousness of God in our lives. We need awareness of the Unchanging and Eternal in times of unusual change and confusion. We need opportunities to confess our failures, shortcomings, and sins, to "wipe the slate clean" for fresh efforts. We need empowerment for the high enterprise of living in dangerous days. We need fellowship with people who have like purposes and needs. Worship can meet these needs. Worship is central in personal religious living. It is of primary importance in the life and work of the church. Without worship personal religion grows weak and the church loses its spiritual power. Worship is unique to religion. Attempts have been made by other agencies in society to take over most of the functions of the church. But the one element in the church's program that remains uniquely her own is worship. If worship goes the church will cease to be the church. The provision of wholesome dynamic worship for its constituency is, therefore, one of the major tasks of the church. The training of young and old in worship is imperative.

How Shall We Worship?—Many churches are searching for a more satisfying pattern of worship. In turning from the extreme forms, symbolism, and ceremonies of the Roman Catholic Church, Protestant churches have moved to an extreme of informal spontaneous worship. It is now generally felt that we need to recover more of the dignity, beauty, and formalism that are native to worship. It is felt also that we must achieve a form of worship that is profoundly sincere and meaningful to modern man. Therefore, fresh study is being made of the whole subject of worship. Certain trends in worship are discernible: the building of more worshipful and appropriate sanctuaries; the placing in well-arranged chancels of the more common symbols of the spiritual life, the altar, cross, candles and the Bible; the more extended use of litanies, prayers, and other liturgical materials; and the disposition to take the art of worship leadership more seriously. We have witnessed in recent years significant developments in the worship programs for children and youth. All of this activity arises from a quickened sense of the importance of worship and the urgent need of making worship a more meaningful experience to those who attend.

Worship is not just a "service," although services must be planned as a common form of providing worship. Genuine worship requires more than skillful leadership, although experience has shown how important effective leadership is to the worshiping congregation. Worship is more than litany, Bible responses, and hymns, yet these are the more common materials of worship. *A worship service represents,* on the human side, *an effort to provide for all persons in the congregation or group the best possible opportunity to realize to the fullest extent genuine fellowship with God and with others.* Just how the service is to be planned, what order it shall follow, what materials shall be used, what acts are to be performed by the leader and the worshiping group, are all questions deserving serious study. Some denominations have well-established practices. For many churches there is no arbitrary standard or ideal in these matters. Our concern here is not to outline a pattern of worship for the church. It is rather to indicate the nature of the problem and to encourage and aid ministers, teachers, and other leaders to approach the matter, not as a problem of the church service primarily, or as pertaining alone to the church school or a given age group, but rather as a function of the entire church.

Planning a Church Program of Worship.—What is greatly needed in the average situation is *a program for meeting the worship needs of all age groups within the church.* There has been considerable confusion in this matter. Many ministers have thought of worship in terms primarily of the Sunday morning "church service." On the other hand, as we have come to emphasize worship in the program of religious education, church school worship services for some ages compete with or become a substitute for their attendance upon the preaching worship service. In most churches we are expecting many people to worship twice within a two-hour period, once in the church school and again in the church service. In scores of churches both services are ungraded. Many who worship in some form in the church school hour and should remain for the church worship service do not do so. These conditions are not satisfactory and do not represent the best provision that can be made.

What is needed is that some representative body in each church, such as the Official Board or the Church Board of Education, should study this problem in its entirety; attempt to determine the type of worship desired in the local church, consider carefully the worship needs of all age groups, and canvass the worship resources of the church, such as, rooms, leaders, size of groups, the degree of gradation desired. Then in the light of these considerations they should plan the total worship program of the church. Such procedure should result in the best possible provision for worship for all age groups in the church in view of all the circumstances and in the light of well-considered aims and principles of worship.

Such a group might well consider the following questions which it is felt must be answered in the attempt to develop a church program of worship. First, what shall be the dominant type of worship for the church as a whole? Second, when and where shall each age group receive its major experience of worship? Third, what other experiences in private devotions and group worship should be provided for each age? Fourth, what training in worship should be provided? If these questions are answered fully and in the most effective manner possible, a church has already in good measure planned its program of worship. The actual plans will vary greatly from church to church, simply because objectives, ideals, and local conditions will vary markedly. Let us now consider these questions with reference to the various age groups.

Planning for the Worship of Adults.—Few churches have a carefully developed program for meeting *all* the worship needs of *all* the adults. Most of them have a number of unrelated worship services occurring on Sunday and during the week. *Where should adults have their major service of worship?* Undoubtedly this should be in the preaching worship service Sunday morning. But most churches have permitted or encouraged a growing emphasis on worship in the church school either in the form of ungraded "opening exercises" or in some type of class or departmental worship. Frequently a "men's brotherhood class" or a large women's class will have their own half-hour worship service. And many of these people will have their worship needs satisfied and will not remain for church. The question naturally arises, why have two worship services for the same people within the two-hour period?

The adult planning committee might well concentrate on making the preaching worship service the central event in the worship of adults. It is led by the minister. Into its planning has usually gone the best materials and preparation. It is attended by more adults than is any other single service. Every effort should be made to secure the full attendance of all adults. Nothing should be allowed to interfere with its appeal and effectiveness. In many churches worship for adults in the church school might be discontinued altogether, or greatly reduced in length. The entire hour could be given over to instruction and other class activities. Where some form of worship for adults does occur in the church school, it should be of an entirely different character from that provided in the church service.

What Additional Worship Experiences Should Be Provided for Adults?—It is entirely possible that some adults cannot, because of home or occupational duties, attend the regular church service. In some churches two identical services at different hours on Sunday are held. To meet the needs of these people and others who may well profit from other worship activities, various types of worship should be considered, such as, prayer meetings, Sunday afternoon vespers, prayer circles, "fellowship cells," and devotional study groups. Careful use should be made of worship opportunities in connection with committee and board meetings, women's society and missionary gatherings. The adult leaders of such organizations should study the needs of their groups and plan accordingly. The total program will doubtless include those seasonal and periodic celebrations that afford opportunity to lift people out of their customary responses and raise their general worship experience to a higher level. In worship training for adults generous use should be made of the devotional sections of the Bible, the hymnal, various prayer manuals, and the growing number of devotional books. The minister may render unusual service in the effort to train people in an understanding, appreciation and practice of worship.

Youth at Worship in the Church.—The church faces a real crisis in making worship meaningful to modern youth. There are many indications that she is doing this none too well. Part of the difficulty is found in the conditions of modern life that seem to render worship unnatural and unattractive to many young people; part of the trouble lies in the mediocre and poorly-planned worship of the church. There is much in current life that makes it difficult for youth to sense a need for and find genuine help in the practice of devotions and group worship. Their lives are increasingly full and complex. Many attractive and easily accessible activities are at hand demanding time and energy. There is little to suggest that they need to "Be still, and know that I am God," or realize that "In quietness and confidence shall be your strength." The scientific temper of the times leads youth to doubt the reality of God and things spiritual; they ask for proof that these things are a vital part of life.

The church's program faces strong competition. An insistent and strong appeal will need to be made to youth on behalf of worship and the devotional life. They must be helped to sense the need of God in their lives and the guidance and strength that may come from worship. Can the church do this? Surely there is the same power and challenge in the Christian religion that has enlisted the response of past generations of youth. Surely no other group has needed more than our youth today the steadying, inspiring

88

experience of fellowship with the Eternal Spirit as a counter-rhythm to the complex and high demanding life they live. Worship may become one of the most salutary experiences of modern young people. The church can and must develop a kind of worship that will minister to an increasing number of youth. All that has just been suggested looking toward better worship in the church will constitute a part of the solution. One of the surest ways to secure a hearty response to the worship of the church is to make that worship attractice, dynamic and rewarding.

Planning the Youth Program of Worship.—Young people may be grouped into older young people, high school youth, and intermediates. The worship needs and program of each group will have much in common and yet they will differ in important aspects. Many leaders feel that it is well for *older young people* to have their worship on Sunday in the preaching worship service. These young people need to be increasingly identified with the adults with whom they are to be associated the rest of their lives. They are sufficiently mature and have a growing body of interests and experiences in common with adults. For these and other reasons it is recommended that the program be so planned that these young people have their major worship experience of the week in the church service. If this decision is made, nothing should be permitted to interfere with their full attendance. Worship for them in the church school hour will be minimized or eliminated entirely. The entire period, as with the adults, might well be used in class discussion.

What additional services· should be planned? Only a committee or the young people themselves in a local church can determine. They may desire to plan and conduct their own informal devotional meeting on Sunday evening. In many churches such a service is part of a larger Sunday evening fellowship meeting. Some groups will plan such a service regularly on a week night. Whenever it occurs it may have genuine value and make a real contribution to the religious life of the group. It provides training in leading worship and enables young people to express their own ideas and preferences. These young people are also entitled to a variety of unusual unique moments of worship. They are responsive to vespers, consecration services, and similar occasions. Such experiences are becoming increasingly a regular part of camp and institute programs and their value to young people cannot be overestimated. Many a youth is lifted to a higher level of worship life and Christian living as a result of such experiences.

High School Youth Worship.—Where may high school youth best worship? There are many leaders who believe that youth of high school age will worship most significantly in services planned and conducted by themselves, which can be better adapted to their needs and interests and which will secure fuller participation. If this is to be the plan in a local church, then every effort and resource should be employed to make graded worship for them a real experience. If this is accomplished then possibly it is not so necessary for them to be urged to "attend church." They have had their Sunday experience of worship. Experience across the country shows that where worship is provided for high school youth in the church school the majority of them do not stay for church.

On the other hand, there is a growing conviction that before these young people go to college or out into the work-a-day world, often breaking away from the home church, they should be brought into close fellowship with the parent church. The criticism seems justified that the graded church school has often failed to bring these young people to relate themselves effectively with the church. Many get "lost" in transfer from the church school to the church. They should be brought as early as seems wise into vital fellowship with their parents and older members of the constituency. Regular participation in the church service is one of the best opportunities of doing this.

Graded worship, or the "opening exercise," in the church school frequently is very poorly planned and conducted. The problems of modern youth referred to earlier suggest that these young people, like their older brothers and sisters, need the most attractive and helpful service of worship the church provides. Many also feel that high school youth are sufficiently mature to share fully in worship with adults. They need the weekly contact with their minister such as the church service affords. In many churches local conditions often make it impossible in graded worship to provide youth with an appropriate room, capable leadership, and a group large enough to experience profitable social worship. These considerations are causing many leaders to feel that high school youth should receive their major worship experience in the preaching worship service.

With respect to additional worship experiences and training in worship, practically all that was suggested for older young people applies to high school youth, only more so! Sunday evening fellowship meetings are quite common with their opportunity for pupil-led devotional services. High school youth, even more than older young people, respond to special services. A wide variety of such services should be a regular part of any church's youth program. Leaders of youth should set themselves persistently and intelligently to train young people in an understanding of the meaning of worship and how to participate and in appreciation of the great hymns, devotional literature, and other materials of worship.

Intermediates, or Junior Hi youth, present more of a problem than the two older groups in that they are less mature and have not developed as much skill in leadership. If they are to worship in a graded service in the church school they will require capable adult leadership. A limited amount of pupil participation in leading is possible. Most churches do not have enough pupils of this age or the facilities and leadership to permit of graded worship. Many of the reasons advanced for providing the major worship experience of high school youth in the church service apply almost as much to Intermediates. Local conditions and the attitude of leaders and the young people themselves will materially influence the decision in a local church. One thing is certain, they must be provided with the best worship the local church can make available.

Worship for Juniors.—The worship of children will be considered with respect to Juniors (age 9, 10, 11) first, and Beginners and Primaries (years 5 through 8) second. The younger children are, the greater is the diversity of abilities and needs from year to year. Grading is extremely important in the children's division. There is a great difference between the worship needs and responses of Juniors and Beginners. Juniors are capable of sustained worship periods. They like some measure of formality, enjoy full participation and are able to read prayers, scripture and other materials. With proper guidance they are capable of exercising some leadership. They respond enthusiastically to opportunities to sing in choirs.

Church school leaders in general favor graded worship for Juniors. Materials may be graded. Leaders acquainted with the needs and limitations of boys and girls may be engaged. Fellowship and informality may be introduced at appropriate times and definite periods of training in worship provided. Their worship may be closely related to the rest of their program. Such a plan assumes, of course, that there are enough Juniors to form a worshiping group and that a proper room is available as well as trained leaders. Where some of these essentials are lacking Juniors will need to worship with other groups. Local conditions, as well as the ideals governing the total program, will determine whether they will worship with some other groups in the church school or be placed in the church service for their major experience of worship. Many ministers encourage Juniors to attend through the use of a Junior choir, children's sermon, and other features. If this is done, it should be carefully related to the total program of the church for Juniors. These boys and girls are responsive to training in the materials of worship. Definite plans for training them in singing hymns, use of scripture, acquaintanceship with the language of prayer, knowledge of religious art and religious symbols should be a part of their worship program.

The Worship of Younger Children.—Beginner and Primary worship will be free, informal and more or less spontaneous. For instance, children may be filled with wonder over a plant that has blossomed or a tiny shoot that has appeared during the week. The wise leader will build a few moments of worship about this observation. Or a child may report the birth of a baby brother or sister and a brief moment of gratitude may be related to the loving kindness of the heavenly Father and the joy of home life. While a good leader will always be prepared to lead children in some form of worship, she will also be on the alert to seize upon such experiences in the lives of children and make them genuinely worshipful.

This means that worship in the Kindergarten and Primary departments will in all likelihood be interwoven with the other aspects of the program more closely than in the case of older groups. Children will move unconsciously from one type of activity to another. Thus it is that a group of children may come into several *moments of worship* during a class session. Those familiar with the development of children's worship during the past few years are acquainted with the large amount of splendid resource material that is available.

No elementary leader need be without helpful selections of hymns, poems, stories, prayers and litanies. Each church should make possible a good supply of such in their library. They can be secured easily and inexpensively in magazines, books, courses of study, and pamphlets.

The rooms and equipment for children's worship is a matter of concern. A rug in some convenient place or chairs that can be brought easily into a fellowship circle represent desirable seating rather than pews or rows of chairs. Blackboards and bulletin boards for worship sentences, pictures and other visual aids to worship will be helpful. It is, of course, highly desirable that each department have a separate room, inasmuch as Beginner and Primary children differ greatly in worship needs and abilities. Such provision is not always possible. A church, however, upon becoming aware of the importance of segregation may make a corner of a larger room available. The use of screens, curtains and bulletin boards assist in reducing distraction and in providing a "home" for the children.

The question naturally arises, should children "attend church"? It has been assumed in this discussion that *when children worship God in their own class or department, that is church to them,* that they are just as truly experiencing worship as are adults in their church service. There are those who feel that children are not "in church" unless they are sharing in the preaching worship service. In some situations it will be necessary for all children to share in this service. There is nothing else for them to do! They must come and go with their parents. There is no other room or service for them. We have already suggested that children's leaders favor graded worship. But where this is impossible and it seems necessary for children to share in the adult service, effort should be made to modify the service to minister more directly to the juvenile members of the congregation. Certainly if children "attend church" regularly for any particular reason, every effort should be made to provide them at some other time with graded experiences of fellowship with one another and with God.

Changing the Sunday Morning Program.—It will be noted that in this chapter we have not attempted to deal in detail with the services of worship for the various ages. Our chief concern has been to raise the questions and treat some of the problems that should be dealt with by workers in the local church as they attempt to *mobilize the total resources of the church in a way to meet most effectively the worship needs of the total constituency.* The church has a great contribution to make to all ages in worship. We must be sure that it is well done. We have recommended that worship in the church school hour for some groups be limited or entirely eliminated in favor of emphasizing participation in the church service of worship. It is possible that the two-period program of the Sunday morning, a one-hour church school and a one-hour church service, is too well established or has too many advantages to be easily modified. And yet there is considerable agitation for and experimentation with different arrangements of the time schedule. Many churches have developed a "Unified Sunday Morning Program," perhaps the most common being a three-session plan, such as the following:

10:00 Class Instruction for All Ages
10:45 Church Worship Service (all ages except the younger children participating; they will have graded services)
11:15 Sermon (when younger members of the congregation retire to their own rooms for additional activity)
11:45 Adjournment for all

Such a plan requires more than one room. Separate rooms for children where they can carry forward their program

95

for the full period would be necessary. Other rooms would need to be available for such groups as Juniors and Intermediates who would retire at the conclusion of the worship service.

Another plan would be as follows:

10:30-11:00	Church Service (with all ages participating)
11:00-11:30	Sermon (with all ages except younger children remaining)
	Class sessions for younger children.
11:30-12:00	Class sessions for all who remained for sermon. Continued session for younger children, possibly featuring graded worship or training in worship.
12:00	Adjournment for all

The length and arrangement of the periods in both plans would be modified to meet local conditions. It should be noted that all members of the family and church constituency may come and go home together, also that the total time spent in the church building might be lessened. There is no particular pattern to be recommended. Again, we need to remind ourselves that our sole concern is that of providing all ages with vital experiences of worship. To do this we need *to use the total resources of the church to meet most effectively the worship needs of the total constituency.*

CHAPTER VIII

INTERPRETING RELIGION

Religion to be properly understood and practiced must be adequately interpreted. This involves instruction and learning. Teaching was preeminent in the religious life of the Jewish community. It had a prominent place from the beginning of the Christian church. It virtually saved Christianity during the dark ages. It was central in the life of the early colonial churches. Out of their passion for teaching religion came the beginnings of higher education in the United States. The Christian church of today faces an imperative task in this field of endeavor. Unless she can organize and carry forward an increasingly effective program of teaching religion to all ages she can scarcely hold her own, let alone become a great evangelizing force.

How Do We Interpret Religion?—The term "teaching" has been narrowly understood. Teaching has been regarded in the past as something that took place primarily in the church school, whereas many forms of instruction at other times were not regarded as part of the teaching program of the church. Such activities as preaching and missionary education, while distinctly educational in nature, have not been effectively related to the instruction that occurred in the church school. Teaching adults in the church school and preaching to them in "church" were regarded as quite different processes and were totally unrelated. It was felt necessary to have a "Missionary Education Sunday" once a month in the church school, as if significant training in the Christian religion could occur without including the spirit and work of missions! This "vivisection" of the total instructional program in the church has been in part responsible for its fragmentary and ineffective nature.

The term "interpretation" of religion is used here purposely to get around the word "teaching" with its traditional meaning and to encourage the broadest possible approach to one of the major functions of the church. By "interpretation of religion" we mean *every effort made by all leaders and agencies in the church to provide for the total constituency a better understanding of the nature and resources of religion for individual and group life*. Such a conception moves beyond the limited understanding and practice of teaching as represented in the traditional Sunday school. It includes, of course, all classes for all ages studying religion on Sunday morning. But it includes also all teaching that occurs in the pulpit, in the various study groups meeting on Sunday afternoon and evening, in missionary and service organizations, in lecture series, in preparatory membership classes, and in forms of teacher-training. Wherever and whenever groups, small or large, in the life of the church meet to seek a better understanding of religion in its broadest sense, teaching or interpreting religion is occurring. Methods of group leadership previously discussed have to do primarily with these teaching-learning situations.

Many Problems Encountered.—Probably more difficulties are found by the average church in this field than in any other. For one reason, a large number of people are engaged in this form of church work. The following comments came from a training conference on instruction and the curriculum: "The courses of study are too difficult for me to handle"; "I feel I simply do not know *how* to teach"; "I have too many different ages in my class"; "I have not thought of my pulpit work as teaching" (this from a minister) ; "The lessons do not interest my pupils"; "Why don't we have more Bible in the courses of study?" "I really do not know what I myself believe about God, Jesus and other things I am supposed to teach"; "We no more than get started in my class before the time is up"; "How may the study of the Sunday evening youth fellowship be related to the Sunday morning instruction?" "The course deals too much with social problems and not enough with 'religion' " ; and so the comments ran. We are all familiar with them.

While we do not solve our problems merely by listing them, nevertheless no solution is made until we carefully analyze them. The more common difficulties in the teaching program may be grouped under the following headings: (1) those centering in an understanding of what teaching is and the organization of a total church program of instruction; (2) those having to do with the selection and presentation of courses of study; (3) special problems of content and interpretation, such as theological beliefs, ways of regarding the Bible; (4) those concerned with teaching procedures, interesting and holding pupils, securing outside preparation; (5) those centering in material factors, such as grading of pupils, size of classes and groups, limitations of time, housing and equipment; (6) those related to the correlation and extension of teaching opportunities, including vacation schools, camps, week day religious instruction. Such a breakdown of the problems affords a group working on them a basis for locating the nature of the difficulties to be dealt with.

With respect to many of these difficulties there is no easy solution. They have always characterized teaching in the church and probably always will. However, ways of dealing more effectively with them can be found. They will require constructive treatment by the committee on education and the teaching staff.

Building a Church Program of Instruction.—The first consideration is the determination of the *scope of the program*. Of what shall it consist? It has been suggested that it should embrace every effort of all leaders and organizations attempting to provide for the total constituency a fuller understanding of religion. Does your committee and staff accept this statement of the scope of teaching? The correlation of all these leaders and agencies presents a long-time task, but it is highly important that those directing the program work steadily at it. One of the first things a group studying the church program should do is to attempt to get a total detailed picture of the fields of teaching. The scope of the program is the first thing to be decided.

Second, *definite aims* should be determined. Selecting objectives involves the emphases and areas of human knowledge and experience to be dealt with in classes and various groups. For instance, how much emphasis is to be placed upon the Bible? Upon social issues? Upon interpreting the church, its history and program? Upon everyday problems of living? Many of these questions are decided by a denomination as it organizes its courses of study for the local church. Yet frequently a church has a choice of courses. And in making these choices it must think through the particular objectives it wants to achieve. Few experiences will make a committee or teaching staff more informed about its curriculum than sharing together in discussion of these matters. This process may become even more meaningful if the leaders of a given age group will work out from time to time the detailed aims for the group by the year and quarter. This really must take place if the instruction is to be most effective.

The International Council of Religious Education has outlined the areas of human experience and knowledge that should form the basis of a curriculum. They are as follow: (1) specifically religious activities; (2) health; (3) education; (4) economic activities; (5) vocations; (6) citizenship; (7) recreation; (8) sex, parenthood and family life; (9) general life in the group; (10) friendship; and (11) aesthetic activities. This list represents a broad approach to the knowledge that may be included in a program of interpreting the meaning of religion for life. The curricula of many of the major denominations have been built largely on this analysis of human experience. And a knowledge of this fact will help local churches to understand better what their editorial offices are offering in the way of courses of study. Other denominations have formed their curricula without any reference to this list. It will be necessary in the last analysis for the local church to determine how narrowly or broadly it will conceive its task of instruction in religion.

The Selection of a Curriculum.—A third consideration will be the actual selection of the courses of study for the Sunday morning session. This is a practical, pressing problem in most local churches. The criticisms reported on earlier in the chapter had to do primarily with this phase of the instructional program. The *first step* in this selection has already been suggested, namely, the determination of the objectives and emphases. Until this is done an intelligent choice cannot be made. A *second step* will be to review carefully the age groups to be served, their distribution into classes, the degree of gradation possible, and the number of classrooms and teachers available. Such facts will have a most important bearing upon the kind of courses to be used. For instance, if classes in the Junior department are formed according to years or grades in school, it will be possible to use closely graded lessons. If the number is small, or for this and other reasons two or three grades must meet together, in all likelihood group graded lessons will be preferred.

A *third step* is to become thoroughly familiar with what

101

your denomination offers for the various ages. Most of us have some information about these offerings. Frequent criticisms are heard about these courses. Some of them are probably justified. But if those inclined to make complaint would first be sure they *know and understand* what the editors and curriculum writers are offering, such criticism might not be made. Every effort is being made by editors and publishers to familiarize local workers with their courses and to interpret and aid in their use. Leaflets describing the courses of study available are to be had for the asking from most denominational publishing houses. In reviewing the courses of study available, the following types of lesson materials will be noted.

Bible Lessons for Christian Living.—This series takes the place of the more familiar and long-used International Uniform Lessons and will be considered especially for older youth and adults. This series is devoted to a survey of the Bible, but the treatment of these Bible passages very often leads the group to the consideration of a wide variety of practical problems of everyday individual and social living. The outlines of these lessons are prepared cooperatively by the denominations acting through the International Council of Religious Education and are released to all denominational boards and independent publishers. For younger groups they are rapidly being supplanted by various forms of graded courses.

The International Group Graded Series.—This series is prepared by a committee of the International Council of Religious Education (on which most of the denominations have their own representatives), is likewise released in outline form to the various editorial and publishing offices. (Some denominations prepare their own outlines.) This series of lessons is organized on the departmental basis, that is, the pupils of all grades within the department will use the lessons for a given quarter at the same time, and thus move through the cycle of three years' work together. They are provided for all ages from Kindergarten through Senior-Young people. The main advantage of these lessons is that they are more suitable for the school in which it is impossible or undesirable to attempt closer gradation. It is also possible to correlate worship and other departmental materials with the lessons from week to week, as well as plan for teacher preparation cooperatively. Some denominations provide no other form of graded lessons for their local church schools, feeling that the majority of the churches cannot use a closely graded series. A careful review of this series will show that the lessons from quarter to quarter cover a wide range of material, treat a number of the areas of human experience mentioned previously, and offer to both teachers and pupils an interesting and informing curriculum. This series is constantly being enriched and supplemented by letters to parents, manuals and magazine treatments. In certain cases two or more denominations cooperate in preparing teaching helps and quarterlies. Some denominations prepare their own group graded lessons.

The Closely Graded Lessons.—These courses are for use in any department that is large enough to grade children very closely, with a separate lesson topic for each class. Such grading follows very closely that of the public schools. There are marked differences between first and third grade children who are usually in a Primary department. Lessons prepared for the first year of the Primary department should be much simpler and adapted to children in their first year of school in contrast with pupils who have already had two years of public school and church school experience. With each year of age the children move to a more advanced body of material. It is felt by many leaders that a closely graded series is the ideal plan, if conditions in the local church permit its use. Here again, most denominations choose topics and material from a wide spread of interests and bodies of knowledge in preparing closely graded series.

Frequently the charge is made that both the group graded and the closely graded courses do not use the Bible as much as do the uniform and other series. It is true they do not use biblical material in quite the same manner. But a careful examination of the graded series will show that they use a remarkably large amount of Bible, as content to be studied, as reference material, as suggested memory and reading assignments, and in other ways. The conviction underlying the organization of these lessons is that there is much knowledge and human experience outside as well as within the Bible that is valuable and highly necessary in bringing children, youth and adults into abundant Christian living. But in no sense is there neglect of this greatest of all source books of religion, the Bible, in the various graded curricula. A great deal depends in the last analysis upon how the lessons are used by those who teach them.

Lessons for the Small Church.—Many denominations have in recent years made special efforts to provide lessons for churches with small enrollment and limited housing. There are many schools that can have no more than four classes—a class for younger children, one for older boys and girls, one for youth and one for adults. Every effort is made to relate the materials closely to the life experiences of those who use them in rural or small town situations. At the same time the basic conceptions of religion, of Christian faith, and of the Bible which are commonly held in these sections are recognized. Special effort is also made to use vocabulary, thought forms and style of writing that are suitable. Simplified teaching procedures and extensive use of stories, Bible material and illustrations are employed.

A careful study of the teacher-leader guidance provided by the various publishing houses will reveal a growing body of helpful suggestions for making the courses of study interesting and profitable. Use is made of not only teacher's quarterlies but also of monthly journals such as *Child Guidance in Christian Living, The Church School Journal, The Baptist Leader, The Highroad*,[1] to carry additional teaching plans and resource materials. Special pamphlets such as *The Adult Student* and *Youth Workshop* [1] provide additional helps for leaders. Never before have teachers and leaders been offered such an array of helpful materials.

Independent and Locally Built Curricula.—Some churches feel that none of these series meets their particular needs. Many denominations and independent publishing houses make available units of study for the various ages that do not necessarily form a part of any organized curriculum. They represent needs that have arisen, constitute reports on unusually fruitful experiences some groups have had, and provide opportunity for studies in special fields. Some such units or texts are much more extended than those of the regular series mentioned above. In some larger churches where leadership is available the committee or staff will prefer to build their own courses of study. This represents a most difficult task and should not be undertaken until the group has thought through on all that is involved and has the resources and leaders to do the work well. It is in a way the most interesting and creative manner of setting up a curriculum for the local church.

Building a Unified Program.—It has been suggested that there are various agencies that may be attempting a teaching program within a given age group in the local church. The question was raised earlier as to the relation of the Sunday morning classes for young people and the evening sessions for that group, or the relation of women's society programs or those of a missionary organization, to the work of adult classes on Sunday morning. Effort is being made to integrate these activities into a unified program of teaching. Denominational educational and editorial boards are attempting to plan together for materials for these various groups in the local church. For instance, the editorial board and the youth department of a given denomination cooperate in selecting topics for both the Sunday morning and Sunday evening meetings of the youth group. They likewise cooperate in selecting materials for vacation and week day class sessions, as well as for the Sunday school sessions, for various ages. Similarly, editorial committees and representatives of denominational missionary boards plan the units of study for adults and young people in local churches somewhat related to the programs for Sunday morning.

Second, the correlation of these various activities for a given age group in a local church is one of the tasks of the local Church Board of Education, or of the Council for a given age group. Here, as well as on a general denominational level, effort can be made to build a unified program of interpreting religion in all its broad aspects. A committee or council on adult work in the local church is the only body that can bring into a unified program the activities of classes, societies, brotherhoods, the sermons from the pulpit, the use of literature and other phases of a total adult program. The same may be true for children and youth.

Leaders in the church may well canvass carefully the various opportunities that may be found in the community for the broader study of religion. Various agencies, and groups, such as a *Learning for Life School, A School of Foreign Affairs, A School of Missions,* a *Leadership Training Class,* or a *Youth Midwinter Institute,* will provide opportunities for instruction beyond what is provided in the local church. Extended use of public and church libraries, reference to religious radio broadcasts, and special lectures are all to be considered.

Time for Instruction.—A great deal of inefficiency and dissatisfaction characterizing instruction in the church is due to limitations of time. We simply cannot do the job Protestantism needs done in interpreting religion on the present time schedule! We can never produce an informed, intelligent constituency upon the basis of the traditional half-hour of instruction common to most church schools. There has been increasing recognition of this fact on the part of a few persons, but the bulk of our church leaders have not yet realized this fact. Until they do and take appropriate action, we will be fighting a losing educational battle. The best of teachers can do only so much within a brief period of time.

Let us face the facts. Most church school programs plan for a half hour of formal instruction on Sunday. And that constitutes their major instructional effort for the week with many, if not most, groups. This limited time is further curtailed in its effectiveness by the poor average attendance of those who are supposed to profit from the teaching. It is further limited by the extensive tardiness characterizing our church school attendance. Still further are the limitations imposed by delays, interruptions, and "special" programs experienced by the average class. If "opening exercises" are held previous to class sessions, they are delayed in beginning and run overtime. Secretaries and others often break into the middle of a class session. Special programs mark the school year, and while often valuable in themselves, they greatly interfere with steady and effective work in the class. These conditions are quite common and constitute more of a handicap to effective work than most of us realize.

These limitations and difficulties support the suggestion made in a previous chapter that if at all possible, worship for many of the groups in the church school hour be eliminated in favor of giving the full hour to instruction. (This with the understanding, as was suggested, that these same groups have their worship in the preaching worship service.) This would give teachers an extended opportunity and also place upon them a heavier responsibility. Certainly most of them would need to make a more thorough preparation in order to lead a class for a full hour. They would also find it possible to plan a much richer and more attractive program of class work.

Providing More Time.—These same considerations as well as other important factors are responsible for the widespread introduction of classes in religion in the week time in connection with the public schools. The conviction is growing over the country, not only among Protestant but also among other religious bodies, that considerably more time must be made available for religious instruction. Furthermore, it is felt that such religious instruction should be more definitely related to the regular program of public education society provides for its young, leading them to see religion as a part of life. Thus it is that in practically every state in the Union such classes have been instituted, calling for the release or dismissal of close to two million school children, to attend classes in religion conducted by the churches. This is a possibility each local church should consider carefully. (See Chapter XII.)

Another significant opportunity to increase the opportunity for religious instruction being embraced by local churches is the vacation church school. Here in several weeks of intensive training the church may provide as much religious instruction as the child normally receives during a year of attendance upon the Sunday church school. Moreover, the long daily sessions, the variety of activities, the intimate association with leaders, together with other features, make the vacation church school a most effective educational program. Usually the minister takes an active part and churches regard the vacation church school as an integral part of the total educational program.

For other age groups the greater use of Sunday afternoon and evening, the holding of special classes, schools, lecture series and conferences during the week time represent current efforts to enlarge the instructional program in the local church. Such activities may be frequent or infrequent, short or long in duration, but in the end they may constitute a significant part of an enlarged program of religious study.

Critical Problems.—In connection with the teaching program of the church certain crucial problems will need to be considered. They will include (1) the attitude toward and place of the Bible in the instructional program, (2) the interpretation to be given to various theological beliefs, and (3) the manner in which the many critical social issues are to be dealt with. Curriculum editors and writers are dealing with these questions continuously. Although many helpful suggestions will come through the courses and program outlines, it is necessary for leaders in the local church to consider these questions seriously. These matters will receive their final interpretation in the pulpit, in class sessions and in other groups in the local church. There may not be complete agreement among workers in the local church with respect to the way the Bible should be regarded and used, religious faith interpreted, and social issues discussed. But their importance in a program of instruction should be recognized and common study of them should result in a more intelligent handling of them in local situations. The Church Board of Education will need to consider them seriously. The minister, because of his position and training, faces an unusual opportunity and responsibility in guiding his teaching associates in their study of these issues.

CHAPTER IX

SOCIAL EDUCATION AND ACTION

Juniors Thinking About War.—A group of Juniors in a certain church became greatly interested in the outcomes of war and peace. The leader very wisely gave them opportunity to follow this interest. They first studied the causes of war. Of course they did not attempt an exhaustive inquiry, but they did consider such causes as: the desire for raw materials, competitive armaments, the "haves" and "have-nots"; rivalries in trade; immigration quotas; desire for territorial expansion; and similar factors. The church school teacher was surprised to learn from the pupils the extent to which the courses in the public school dealt with these matters. The children then undertook to outline some of the ways to prevent the outbreak of war. They became familiar with such terms as treaties, trade agreements, tariffs, International Bank, The United Nations Organization, Conscientious Objectors, the Four Freedoms. They sent a delegation to hear a sermon by the pastor on "Christ or Mars" and the report was made the basis for a lively discussion. They interviewed such authorities as they could contact. They secured some of the literature available.

A final step led them to consider what they could do. One of the practical projects undertaken was the construction of a set of posters expressing their opposition to war as a means of settling international disputes and outlining specific ways of working for peace. As people came to church one Sunday morning they were confronted by these posters, by means of which the children presented their ideas and sought to influence their elders. It made quite an impression on the church and led to many discussions on the part of the adults. Parents learned what their children were thinking and table and fireside talk took on a more serious tone. Another project undertaken was to prepare letters to be sent to congressmen expressing their views. Some of these letters were published in the local paper. A group of children had experienced social education and action.

Young People Tackling a Problem.—A group of young people in a midwestern city became quite aroused over the ejection of Negroes from one of the public eating houses. Their leader wisely suggested that they secure an accurate picture of the local situation before attempting any action. A visit to the restaurant was planned. A frank talk with the manager followed his first attempt to get rid of them as "nuisances." For one thing they learned that the manager's attitude was due, not to personal prejudice, but rather to a knowledge of what the majority of his white patrons would do if the practice of permitting Negroes to eat there persisted. The young people inquired into the situation of other eating house owners. They discovered a common agreement among them as to policy, as they claimed, "all in the interest of self-protection."

The young people then undertook to canvass adult sentiment on the matter, beginning first with people in the churches of the community. While the study was not exhaustive they discovered that a high percentage of the "Christians" were opposed to promiscuous sharing on the part of colored people in the restaurants of the community. This discovery caused great concern on the part of the youth. Were their Christian elders justified in such a position? If not, what could they do about the question? They consulted

111

with their pastor. They found that he had investigated the situation some time in advance of their study. They were led to recall the sermon he had preached some months previously on the subject, and the protests that some members registered against his "liberal" stand. He urged persistence in their effort to bring about a change of attitude and practice on the part of the public, but cautioned patience and careful procedures.

After spending several weeks in studying the literature on the subject, especially instances of dealing with the same problem in other communities, several steps were decided upon. (1) Another sermon by the minister was suggested, to be followed by a general discussion on the following Wednesday evening. (2) An open letter to the restaurant owners of the community to be published in the paper, not primarily condemning them but calling upon citizens to support them in a more liberal practice. (3) Young people teamed up as individuals and small groups to take their Negro friends to eat with them in the eating places. (4) Joint study with their Negro friends of this and related problems of Negro-White relations in recreation, social life and kindred problems in the community.

Adults in Action.—During the war a group of Christian adults in a city church undertook to help locate several Japanese-American families in their community, in spite of strong opposition on the part of many people. Among other things they attempted to change the attitude of people as they met them in various social occasions, whenever hostility and prejudice were shown. They sought to introduce the Japanese to people in their church and community. They canvassed the community for houses. In two instances Japanese families were housed with some of their number until homes could be found. They challenged the restrictive covenants of the real estate companies. In spite of criticism and opposition they endeavored to express throughout what they considered to be their patriotic and Christian duty. Christian adults were in action.

Importance of Social Education and Action.—Churches and individual Christians are increasingly concerned to make our social order more Christian. The 20th century will undoubtedly go down in history as the time of a "great social awakening," the "birth of the social gospel." This really means that large numbers of Christians and churches sense the imperative necessity of changing conditions in society that adversely affect individuals and are at variance with the spirit and teachings of Jesus. If this is to be done effectively it will require that the church carry forward a strong program of education and action that will touch every important social issue and include all ages. One of the functions of the church previously listed is "to provide opportunity and training for individuals to participate in efforts to improve society."

Social education and action therefore must become a vital part of the program of Christian education in the local church. It is particularly important that children and youth be made keenly aware of the problems and evils of society and be enlisted and trained in efforts to make their environment more Christian. It cannot begin too early in life, for social attitudes and habits form quickly. Whenever children are old enough to notice differences between themselves and those of a different color, race, religious faith, or economic status, they are old enough to sense the way in which adults regard these differences. They are excellent imitators. We must prevent them from imitating the prejudices, fears, and limited outlook of the adults surrounding them and develop in their lives more truly Christian attitudes and practices than those characterizing their elders.

Adults find themselves in a dynamic world. New problems

113

and situations confront them constantly. There is nothing static about modern society. This means that men and women must constantly study their social environment, bringing it under the criticism of Christian ideals and standards. They must attempt to make ever more effective the spirit and teachings of Jesus as the very leaven of society. Never before has there been such widespread educational effort among adults as exists at present. The church has a great stake in this matter. She believes that only Christianity has the ultimate solution. Her adult constituency must be kept alert, informed, and active with respect to the major social issues and programs of social betterment.

Personal Faith and the Social Gospel.—Frequently the "social gospel" is set off in sharp distinction from "personal religion" as if a choice must be made between the two. Such is not the case. Personal Christian living is basic to a Christian society. Vital personal religious experience and faith are absolutely essential on the part of those who seek to change social conditions. It is increasingly felt also that one cannot be a real Christian without concern for the condition of our social environment. Both the personal and the social gospel are involved in complete Christian living. Neither is an elective in the Christian way of life. Jesus made this very clear in his statement of the two great commandments. "Thou shalt love the Lord thy God . . . and thy neighbor as thyself." Who is my neighbor? Jesus answered that question for all time with the unforgettable story of the Good Samaritan. Who are our neighbors? Those in need! And they are all about us. The alleviation of suffering, the righting of social wrong, the correction of evil conditions that adversely affect any of our "neighbors" is our Christian duty. We have been tardy in recognizing the full implication of the second great commandment as interpreted by Jesus.

What Are the Social Issues?—These issues may be variously stated. Among them the following would certainly be listed: (1) Economic problems, including profits, wages, strikes, security, and access to the physical resources of the entire earth. (2) Race relations, including equality of opportunity on the part of all to secure the essentials of living, brotherhood and cooperation. (3) Nationalism, involving questions of sovereignty, cooperation, internationalism. (4) War, its causes, costs, armaments, and ways to peace. (5) Liquor and narcotics, their manufacture, distribution and attendant evils. (6) Divorce and the breakdown of the home. (7) Ignorance, sanitation, disease and sickness.

Each of these barriers to the realization of God's will on earth may be broken down into a number of important aspects. Any group undertaking serious study might well make its own analysis of the issues and problems confronting society today. These issues will not challenge all individuals and groups alike. Some will seem to be more serious or offer greater opportunity for action than others. In some localities certain problems or issues will naturally be of more immediate concern because the local conditions force them to the attention of the people. Something has to be done about them immediately. Yet it is highly important that all Christians be made keenly aware of these issues and what is involved in their solution, whether or not they present difficulties in their environment close at hand.

Procedure in Social Education and Action.—Anyone undertaking or directing social education and action will need to be familiar with certain steps that experience has proved to be necessary.

First, *get the issue or problem clearly defined*. One cannot move intelligently to solve a problem unless that problem is clearly and accurately seen. Take, for instance, the race problem. What are the major issues involved? How may they be most helpfully stated? What are the basic attitudes of repre-

115

sentatives of the races involved? How do these attitudes depart from Christian and democratic conceptions of racial differences and relations? What discrimination is being practiced and against whom? What is the exact nature of the tensions between races? What are the hopeful and constructive aspects of the situation?

Second, *secure accurate and full information*. It is at this point that individuals and groups often fail. They are unable or unwilling to make the effort to secure the facts in the case. They rely on hearsay, rumor, propaganda, or mere opinion. One of the greatest dangers is that those who would do good will act upon incomplete or erroneous information. They may do more harm than good. There must be insistence upon taking the time and making the effort to gather all information attainable before plans for action are initiated. Fortunately, reliable information is becoming increasingly available so that any group that seeks guidance may secure it. Books, pamphlets, magazines, informed persons are to be found in ever-increasing volume. It is particularly important that we become skillful in recognizing reliable data, that we learn how to detect propaganda, that we secure information on all sides of a question. Those who attempt to inform and lead children and youth will be agreeably surprised at the amount and usable form in which information on the great social issues is being made available for children and youth in public schools and other ways.

There are many opportunities in the church for educating people, young and old, on social problems. Consider the following as suggestive: sermons by the minister, church school classes, church night sessions, teacher training classes, conferences, institutes and summer camps, reading courses, library provisions, literature tables, studying the community calendar for instructional periods outside the church. The public schools, service clubs, women's organizations, business groups, as well as the wide range of newspapers, magazines, and radio programs all offer unusual opportunities for the alert individual and church to supplement the training given in the church.

Third, *form opinions and make decisions*. Information does little good unless it is used to develop a point of view. It is essential that we carry the study of facts and the interpretation of information to the point where we arrive at definite decisions. Many Christians stop short of this and hence never go into action. This is a difficult step. Questions seem to have two sides. Equally sincere persons may be ranged on both sides. The matter of judgment always enters in. Some questions appear to be so involved that we feel we never entirely encompass them in our thinking. And yet the time comes when we must leave off "thinking about things" and "do something" about them. Votes must be taken and counted. Many decisions will need to be of a somewhat tentative nature, awaiting further information or testing in action.

Such information as we seek to provide must somehow connect with the emotional and volitional side of the individual. Many people "think with their emotions" and often thinking is mistakenly taken to be the "rearrangement of one's prejudices." Nevertheless we seldom act unless we are "stirred" to move. Therefore, in social education it is highly important that we broaden the outlook, arouse social imagination, quicken social sympathy, and extend the social interests of people. It is usually thus that people are moved to action.

In many cases it will be found that common agreement on points of view and plans of action cannot be reached. It will be necessary for part of the group to take one course of action, the rest to follow another. Sincere majorities cannot disregard equally conscientious minorities. Each group must be permitted to speak for itself. It is highly important that in the church we attempt to keep unbroken the bonds of

Christian fellowship, even though we differ sharply among ourselves. It will be likely that some small pioneering groups will go beyond the point of view and commitment of the large body of church members. While the smaller groups cannot speak for the entire congregation, neither should they be denied the privilege of expressing in word and action *on their own behalf* their conviction. Here is the real test of Christian fellowship and democracy. We have been all too slow in learning how to practice both democracy and true Christian fellowship within the church in times of crisis.

Fourth, *plan and execute a program of action.* This is the culminating step. It is the ultimate test of our Christianity. The constant complaint of the early Christians running throughout the gospels and letters of the New Testament is not that people did not know what to do, but that they failed to do what they knew they ought to do. This is equally true of modern Christians. It is essential that we first plan carefully what we intend to do in the area of social action. There are ways *and* ways of going into action. Much attention needs to be devoted to the strategy of working for human betterment. We want to help the poor. How may this be done most effectively and with the most benefit to those who receive? We are definitely opposed to corruption in government, but how can this opposition be constructively expressed? Next to our failure to secure full information, our lack of effective methods of attacking social evils has been our greatest weakness. Recent years have witnessed not only the release of vital information but also the development of methods, technics and associations for social action. Instead of sporadic and miscellaneous giving, we have organized charity which discovers real need and develops ways of giving that build up self-respect and self-reliance in those who receive. Many agencies have been formed through which wise and effective action may be taken to work for the abolition of war and the establishment of permanent peace. Within many of the denominations boards and commissions are available for counsel. Interpretations of crucial issues and Christian programs of action are recommended. Any individual or group disposed to enter on a course of action would do well to survey the field, within and outside the church, to discover what groups of similar purpose exist and how one may associate with them in action.

A Church Program of Social Action.—What has been said in this chapter applies to *all* age groups. Many projects of social action will be planned with respect to the limitations and needs of various age groups. The curriculum outlines for children and youth usually include numerous units dealing with various problems of society. The minister and church boards will deal with them from time to time. Special interest groups will arise to follow through on some issues. It would be highly desirable that these various approaches and activities be brought into the unity of a total church program. Emphases throughout the church, from sermon to Beginners department, on race relations, wages, causes of war, family relations, or any other vital social issue might be more effective in outcomes if carried throughout the church at the same time. It would make possible cooperation in training among parents and all leaders in the church. It would afford content for family discussion, make possible the use of all the resources that might be assembled, and provide opportunity for all, young and old, to participate in united, church-wide action. Leaders must be urged and aided to plan training and develop projects adapted to the limited understanding and abilities of children. In addition to whatever contribution such action would make to worthy causes, it would serve to bind people of all ages together in a rich, vital fellowship as members of a local church.

Pioneering Leaders Needed.—A thoroughgoing emphasis upon social action will require much of leaders. Teachers cannot take pupils where they themselves have not gone. Theoretical study of and lip service to Christian social ideals will not be enough. It will be necessary for workers with all ages to move into the "front line trenches" of social endeavor, to become pioneers in applying Christian teachings to the social evils of our day. The kind of authority most Christian leaders need in influencing others grows out of a knowledge that such leaders are unafraid to "stand up and be counted" for truth and righteousness under all circumstances, that they are willing to risk much to advance human welfare some. The same requirement will need to be met by parents. All that has been said previously about the influence of parents and the home environment needs to be recalled here. Alert, conscientious, Christian parents can do more than any other single group to shape the social attitudes and practices of the growing generation. Many Christian leaders and parents, conscientiously striving to follow where the Master led in self-forgetting service, have experienced their deepest sense of comradeship with Christ in sacrificial service and suffering. Discipleship to Christ would become vastly more meaningful to multitudes of Christians if they entered more fully into the "fellowship of mourning" with Christ over conditions that oppose the coming Kingdom of Love and Righteousness.

Chapter X

Christian Nurture in the Home

"The family is the foundation of human fellowship. Marriage is not to be entered into unadvisedly, but reverently, discreetly, and in the love of God." So reads the marriage service. "Home religion" has been in past decades a mighty influence in the religious nurture of the young. There are many indications at the present time that the home is failing to meet its share of responsibility in Christian education. The struggle to make society Christian will undoubtedly be lost or won in the homes of the country. A clarion call is going out in these days to parents to accept their inescapable responsibility and high privilege in caring for the religious nurture of their children.

Threats to the Modern Home.—Each generation of parents undoubtedly has felt that they were working against greater odds than parents ever before faced. Certainly this is true of the present generation. And in many ways there is justification for their reaction. While there are vastly more aids to modern parents in their nurture of the young than previously, there are also some real threats to religion in the home that arouse deep concern. Sociologists, educators, religious leaders, medical men and many others are well aware of this fact. The danger spots in modern life are well known. The following may be mentioned as among the most serious: the mounting divorce rate and the consequent increase in broken homes; absentee parents with the resulting neglect of children and the impoverishment of home life; rapidly changing home-sites and the consequent insecurity for countless numbers of children; the increased consumption of alcoholic drink and its attendant evils; sheer ignorance of and indifference to child nurture and guidance of the young on the part of countless numbers of fathers and mothers; absorption of parents in recreational, cultural and other activities outside the home with resulting neglect of home-making relationships and activities; and gross religious and biblical illiteracy characterizing multitudes of parents rendering them incapable of giving religious nurture to their children. Life today is dynamic, full of rapid change and unexpectedness, putting extra strain upon both parents and children in everyday living. Alongside this rather disturbing picture must be noted the great increase in the number of agencies and facilities now available to parents in enriching home life and in the better training of their children. The total situation represents a curious mixture of great dangers to and tremendous possibilities for nurture in the home.

Statesmanlike Planning Needed.—Protestant churches must engage in a special effort to enlist and train parents in the important business of home-building and child nurture. The activities of the various denominations and of such agencies as the International Council of Religious Education are testimony to the fact that statesmanlike planning is under way. The number of conferences and schools being held and the wide variety of books, magazines, and other literature being published indicate the seriousness with which this problem is being dealt with. There will be no adequate solution to the problems encountered in this field until the churches are able to "grow a generation of parents" who are capable of providing the religious nurture required in modern life. In the meantime, however, religious leaders should utilize every means possible to help today's parents to discharge their responsibilities as effectively as possible. Among the emphases being developed in the present program of the churches are the following: training for youth in preparation for marriage and parenthood, guidance of young married couples and new fathers and mothers, provision of parent associations and other forms of fellowship and mutual helpfulness in the church, guidance in the realization of basic values of democracy and religion in the home, and cooperation between parents and teachers of youth in the church. In addition, churches are endeavoring to work with other agencies in society that are concerned with family welfare in strengthening their work and in making their services available to their own members.

Preparing Youth for Marriage.—The approach to the problems of courting, marriage and parenthood is today much more open and wholesome than in preceding generations. These fundamental experiences of life are dealt with frankly, honestly and constructively. Surely many of the problems incident to courting, love-making, engagements, and marriage should disappear as youth come more to see these things in their true relationships and are given counsel and guidance as they deal with them in real life. One of the areas of human experience taken into account in curriculum making by most denominations is that of "preparation for marriage and parenthood." Units of study and various materials become a part of the church's program for youth by which they are given help in these matters. The pastor or adult counselor or parent who can gain the confidence of youth, keep in close touch with them as they meet the problems in this area, will find himself entering into ever more helpful relationships with them. A great ministry to young people is possible at this point by church leaders and Christian parents if they are alert and prepared to aid. The least such adult leaders can do is to make youth acquainted with the helpful literature and conferences and classes now available.

Helping Youth Build a Home.—In days when divorces and broken homes are so common, the church may render a great service by leading young people to sense the sacredness of the marriage vow, the seriousness of establishing a home and its sanctity in society, and the tremendous responsibility of bringing children into the world. Such attitudes may seem old-fashioned and outmoded. Yet they are foundation stones of successful home life. Few things are better able to counteract the growing disposition in society to treat lightly these great life experiences. Marriage in the church, with a clergyman officiating, with every element of religious significance attached to the event in the lives of two people is highly desirable. The importance of this relation to the church is sensed when we realize that the church is the only institution in society that attends the individual throughout his earthly pilgrimage. It has blessed the marriage of his parents before he was conceived. It greets him at birth and cherishes the privilege of christening him and enrolling him in the nursery-home department. It stays by and helps train the parents during those years when his life is confined almost entirely to the four walls of the home. It welcomes him to its life and fellowship as soon as he is able to share activities with others. It follows him through life as he passes through various stages of development, always ready to encourage, counsel, comfort, train and enrich his life, and then asks the privilege of saying a prayer over his lifeless form as it is lowered into the grave. No other agency in society attempts such continuous contact and renders such a ministry as the church. Marriage therefore should be blessed by the church and performed by an ordained minister.

Aiding the Young Parent.—The significance of the early years of life is now generally recognized. It is commonly believed that the first five years of a child's life are more determinative of his character and personality than any other comparable period. Hence it is that schools, churches and other agencies are giving increasing attention to aiding parents in meeting the problems and opportunities of nurture during these formative years. Many churches form mother's circles for the discussion of common problems and other forms of self-education. Occasional meetings with the fathers present ought to be planned. Literature covering each year of growth and practically all aspects of the child's development is available, much of it in brief, inexpensive form. Appropriate story material, prayers, songs, and pictures are easily available to parents. The first courses of the church school, especially in nursery and kindergarten departments, have manuals that are prepared as much for parents as for teachers. A classic example of this is Lloyd's *Religious Nurture in Nursery Class and Home*.[1] These beginning courses usually have guidance material and letters that go to the home to assist parents in their part in the program. Such magazines as *The Christian Home*[1] provide help to parents of a varied and practical nature.

Parent-Church Guidance of Youth.—If the cooperation suggested for the early years can be maintained throughout the child's growing experience in the church, we are assured of a much more effective program of religious nurture. That this is neither established nor continued through adolescence is the sad truth about many churches. And the total program of religious education is correspondingly ineffective. Protestantism will never be able to do for its children what it should until there is wholehearted and intelligent cooperation between parents and those working in the church school. Such cooperation may be furthered in such ways as the following: (1) through parent participation in program planning; (2) through parents taking part in teaching and leading in various activities; (3) through a parent-teacher association; (4) through letters and other communications from churches to the homes; (5) through parent training classes and conferences; (6) through counseling on the part of the minister and other adult workers in the program, especially as serious situations arise in individual homes; (7) through shared programs and social gatherings, such as a class or department having their parents with them for a Sunday or week night social event or demonstration of their work. These and many other similar activities are becoming more common as churches and parents alike realize their significance in the total program of Christian nurture. Leaders in the church and parents should confer much more readily and continuously over problems and needs affecting individual pupils. Any alert group of teachers and parents will discover ways of building more helpful cooperation in their local situations.

"The Family in the Church."—There is growing recognition of the value of having the family share as such in various activities in the church. There has been too much of a tendency to break down family solidarity in the church. The relation of children to the regular church worship service was discussed in Chapter Seven. While it will be advisable to have children grouped alone for certain activities, it is increasingly felt that the family should share together, at least occasionally, in worship, as well as in some other phases of the program just referred to. In many churches, especially in rural sections, this is already happening. Church night programs, frequently including a "pot-luck" dinner, group singing, and games that all ages can participate in, offer splendid opportunity for family sharing. Parties, picnics, seasonal programs, such as Christmas, Thanksgiving, Easter, exhibits, and demonstrations of on-going program activities in class and department, are among the things that may bring children, youth and parents together in the church. Total family life and loyalty that centers in the church is highly desirable.

What Makes Home Life Religious?—Parents are more eager for an answer to this question than any other. First of all, they need to understand how broad and inclusive religion is as it finds full expression in the home. The prevalent idea that it means primarily or solely family devotions and grace at meals is utterly inadequate. It is a quality that must permeate all the life, relationships and activities of the home. Churches need to help parents relate religion to the home in the following ways.

Religion finds expressions through the attitudes, ideals and practices of the parents. Here as elsewhere, "what you are speaks so loud I cannot hear what you say." A modern philosopher declared, "I got my religion from my mother who never talked religion to me." He absorbed, "caught" it from her God-filled, Christ-illumined daily living. Charles Lamb once said, "I am resolved to bring my children up in the religion of their father,—if they can discover what it is"! Children are affected far more by the attitudes of their parents toward life in general, toward others, toward the church and toward God than by anything else. Parents who attempt to teach one thing and live something else simply "can't get away with it" before their children. Often children of professedly religious parents turn from the church because the lives of fathers and mothers do not ring true. It is likewise true that children of very humble parents who do not make much of a profession before the world become faithful and loyal Christians because of the quality of religious living they observed daily in their home life. What a parent believes in and is devoted to cannot long remain hidden from a child.

Learning Religion Through Democracy in the Home. —The Christian religion and democracy have much in common. They both seek to realize in the lives of all certain great personal and social values. These include a sense of personal worth, respect for others, willingness and ability to work with others for common ends, response to duly constituted authority, observance of the "rules of the game" in all cooperative activity, a feeling of good will toward others, loyalty to the highest purposes sought by the group. Where these values and relationships are experienced by the members of the group, there religion is finding true expression. "The family is that relationship of parents and children, initiated and fostered by creative interaction, which generates, individualizes, and integrates personality, on the one hand, and promotes the growth of culture in the community on the other hand. God is creativity of Life which speaks to us through this creative interaction. God is this creative love that promotes growth. . . . Religion is that way of living which gives God the most important place in all situations." [2]

In many homes parents have attempted to inculcate religion without realizing in any way the values and relationships we are here describing. Whatever else religion may mean in the home, it must find expression in the form of gracious, happy cooperative planning, sharing, and participating in the democratic way of life. There must be respect for the judgment of younger members, the right to be heard and have a voice, respect for property, even that of the smallest child, shared responsibility in meeting the duties and responsibilities of home work, and all the other things that enter vitally into family living.

Religion a Matter of Family Conversation.—Greater effort is being made to center conversation in the home in topics and problems related to religion. Most families discuss in one way or another some of the stirring events of the day, or are brought face to face with issues on which they are compelled to take sides. Here are opportunities to bring to bear upon current problems the teachings of religion and the

church, as individual members of the family try to form attitudes and think through to courses of action. If "honest-to-
goodness" efforts are made by various members of the family
to live as real Christians in the midst of the perplexing world
situation, there certainly will be need for counsel together and
community of action which will inevitably assume a religious
nature and create bonds of Christian fellowship unknown
before. The religious life of multitudes of families is im-
poverished because they are not living deeply, earnestly, and
sacrificially. One of the ways to make religion vital to home
life will be to try to find guidance, strength and help in
dealing with the major issues life presents today as well as
in solving problems of personal and family living. There is a
vast difference between the home where religion and the
church are considered casually or critically or not at all and
the home where they are central in the thought and life of all
its members.

Religion Finds Expression through Worship.—There
is concern over the seeming decline in family devotions and
grace at meals. It is difficult to know the extent to which such
practices are on the decline. Since family worship and table
grace have been so prominent in church homes of the past,
it raises the question as to what are to be the modern substi-
tutes if they are outmoded. There is no guarantee that such
practices will promote the religious attitude, yet it is true that
many of us who grew up under their influence feel that they
made a great contribution to our religious development.
There seems to be at the present moment a revival of interest
in such activities in the modern home. Perhaps the pattern
is not so routine and rigid as that of the past, but parents are
sensing the importance of relating God more intimately to the
totality of home interests, problems, joys and sorrows. In
addition to regular times of family meditation, occasions are
sought when the family may naturally gather about the

piano for a sing, celebrate a festival, rejoice together in a birthday, commemorate a special family event, or meet a great crisis or sorrow, introducing into such moments a strong and wholesome religious note. Most families find children and youth respond enthusiastically and that "it does something" to family fellowship. Literature and similar helps are increasingly being made available for such activities.[3]

When Are Parents Teaching Religion?—All the time and in all kinds of relationships and situations they are teaching. Often they do not realize it. When parents fail to get up on Sunday morning in time for church school does that teach children anything? Yes; simply that in their opinion religion and the church are not worth the effort of getting up in time. When parents openly and unduly criticize their minister and the church is that doing anything to the children? Yes, it is inculcating attitudes of criticism and disloyalty. When parents make slighting remarks about those of another race or refuse to fellowship with them are they teaching? As surely as boys and girls are apt to absorb the attitudes and follow the patterns of the living of their parents. When parents give meagerly and grouchily to the support of the church they are revealing to their children what they really care for. Such action speaks with greater influence than anything they may say. So it is, there is no escaping the great responsibility resting upon parents *to live their religion* and *to share their struggles to live religiously with their children.* They are their children's real teachers of religion!

"At the close of a day a father and mother with their children were watching a sunset, and its reflection on a mountain lake. . . . The colors and whole effect were beautiful, and not even the children broke the quietness of the moment, until the little three-year-old said, as he took his father's hand, 'Daddy, let's say the blessing.'

"This response from a very little child did not just happen. It came from the natural inclusion of God our Father in the everyday life of the family. The child had unconsciously breathed the atmosphere of a home where God was the center. Father and mother and children were all fun-loving and wholesome. 'Grace' was, of course, said at the table. There was family worship in which little children could participate. There were bedtime stories and prayer. In all such expressions the Bible had its place. In helping their children to know God, parents must themselves know and love him and relate all of life to his purposes." [4]

CHAPTER XI

DEVELOPING CHRISTIAN LEADERS

The genius of Protestantism has been in part its use of lay people in leadership in its program. The traditional Sunday school was a layman's organization. During the past 150 years the teaching of religion has been largely in the hands of lay people. It is to the glory of the Sunday school that it has been maintained through the decades primarily through their services. Leadership in educational work is one of the most exacting and difficult tasks in the church. Yet in spite of this, the largest number of people identified with a specific task in the local church is engaged in church school work. It is a testimonial to the motivating power of the Christian religion that it has enlisted the interest, enthusiasm, and continuing service of so large a body of Christians in such work.

Broadened Conception of Leadership.—The program of religious education in the local church as it has been interpreted in the foregoing chapters calls for a broader understanding of leadership. We are concerned with *all workers who are serving the church in any special capacity*. We have interpreted the educational program as educational method applied to the entire task of the church. When such activities as fellowship and recreation, visitation and counseling, worship and training in the devotional life are embraced in the program along with instruction, it naturally involves a wide spread of leaders. We need to develop capable trained leaders for *all* phases of the church's program. Stewards, deacons, official board members, and leaders of women's organizations are to be afforded opportunities for training as well as teachers and departmental superintendents of the church school.

Types of Leaders Needed.—The range of talents and abilities needed in the broad program of the church is appreciated only when one attempts to make a complete list of them. In addition to "teachers and officers of the church school" it includes: secretarial workers; visitors; stewards; musicians; song leaders; librarians and literature secretaries; publicity specialists; deputation team leaders; recreational leaders; workers with hobbies, handcraft and other forms of creative activity; chairmen and officers of boards and committees; cooks and caterers; social case workers; family visitors, counselors; and educational supervisors. Each local church should make its own list of services to be rendered. That church is experiencing wholesome spiritual and material growth that engages the talents and loyalty of a large number of people in its program.

Discovering Workers.—Only as the full range of types of leaders is kept before us are we in a position to match needs with potential leaders. Much talent goes unused in churches simply because it is not discovered and the need for it is not clearly presented. The minister or church board that keeps these types of service freshly in mind as the total membership of the church is reviewed will be better able to locate the persons fitted for such services. The minister of a medium-sized church was found with his membership roll open before him on the desk. On charts around the walls of the room were listed the various types of service for which leadership was needed. As he went through this membership roll he considered each person with respect to his special talents, services now engaged in and possibilities of further service—and the names were placed in appropriate columns.

133

Only thus could he be sure he had discovered the potential leadership in his church. Such a careful canvass does not of itself guarantee that all positions will be filled, but it will be found far more effective than the absence of any systematic plan.

Enlisting Workers.—Doubtless the most difficult aspect of the whole leadership problem is that of enlisting and motivating people to serve. It is true that with large numbers of volunteers little external motivation is necessary to secure their services. They seem willing and even eager to do their part. Yet what church does not at times cast about for a few more workers? Some churches are desperately seeking leaders. Often the question comes, what is wrong with modern religious education that it is so difficult to enlist workers? Rather the question should be, what is wrong with the average Protestant church? Is it failing to *teach* and *preach* a religion that motivates people to faithful and sacrificial service? Whenever it is found difficult or impossible to man the program, such a situation is in part a reflection upon the spiritual life of the church. Pastors and other leaders need to study carefully effective methods of securing commitment of lay people to the tasks of the church. Various appeals will need to be made: love of God, devotion to Christ, concern for the success of the church, the appeal of people in need, love of working for others, loyalty to the pastor, satisfaction in participating in group activity, responsibility for working at the unfinished tasks of the kingdom. Individuals will not all respond alike. The motive that will move some will not appeal to others.

Those attempting to recruit workers need to realize that there are many factors rendering the task unusually difficult today. The lives of people seem to be so much more crowded than they used to be. Entertainment and cultural activities are claiming the time and energy of people. Many types of worthy community service are calling for volunteers. In addition, the work of the church, especially educational work, is increasingly exacting. Such leadership requires preparation. Pupils expect more of their teachers today. Church workers are in a sense competing with better trained leaders in public schools, clubs and other community agencies. The children, youth and adults the church is attempting to reach are finding strong appeals to their interests in the many entertainment and cultural activities now available. All of these things constitute stiff competition with the efforts the church is making. We will need to be ever more skillful and persistent in our efforts to enlist and train men and women in Christian service.

Training the Leaders of the Church.—The church must realize that there is no alternative to undertaking thorough, continuous leadership education. That churches have not realized this is indicated by the fact that so many churches make no consistent efforts along this line. Multitudes of willing workers are continuously without opportunity to improve themselves as leaders. It will be necessary to canvass and utilize a wide variety of training activities, such as: teacher training classes and schools, church night series, workers' conferences, institutes, literature and reading courses, observation, apprenticeships, personal conferences, summer schools, correspondence courses, and supervision by experienced and trained leaders. The effort of the various denominational boards and of the International Council of Religious Education have resulted in a wealth of suggestions, a wide variety of resources and materials, and a growing body of people capable of helping to train others. With the resources and experience now available, *no church should be without a strong program of training*. No workers, regardless of how remote or isolated the location, should be beyond assistance in becoming better trained.

Christian Character and Experience Foremost.—
Leaders in the church should possess strong Christian character and know religion from personal experience. The more fully we understand the basic processes of Christian nurture, the more we realize the importance of the personality of the leader and his personal experience of religion. Leaders cannot interpret what they themselves do not know. They cannot take people out onto the frontiers of Christian endeavor without themselves living in the danger zones of Christian idealism and practice. The "authority" the Christian leader of today needs is the same kind of authority that preeminently characterized the life of Jesus. He "spake as never man spake before"; he practiced his most exacting precepts daily; he was a living demonstration of his own "way of life." People today, baffled, confused, misled, young and old, are seeking for authoritative leaders who can point the way. Never have those who attempted to point the way faced a more difficult task. Yet never before has there been such a magnificent opportunity to give guidance and render service. The Christian church bears a heavy responsibility to provide that kind of leadership.

How are such leaders produced? Essentially they must grow out of the life of the church. They must be the products of Christian homes. There is no other source from which they may come. There is no shortcut in the development of such leaders. The most important aspect of any church program for developing leaders is in the last analysis to be found in the immediate environment in which the potential leaders live. The quality of the home life, the spiritual richness of church worship, the helpfulness of the instruction and preaching, the influence of strong Christian personalities, the attitudes and motives toward humanitarian service, the warmth and contagion of fellowship, these are among the elements that eventually determine the kind of leaders that arise in the church.

The Leadership Training Program.—We have already indicated the various training activities that may be introduced. Through these means special insights and skills are added to qualities of Christian character and experience in producing the kind of leaders needed. The local church should consider all of these means carefully and experiment to discover those that will meet local needs. Experience has shown some to be more serviceable than others. These will be briefly discussed here.

(1) *The Workers' Conference.* The most frequently recurring form of training is doubtless the monthly teachers' meeting or Workers' Conference. Multitudes of churches are using these meetings as genuine training situations. Topics and problems are discussed, speakers are scheduled, programs are outlined and criticized, books and other literature are read and reported upon. Ten or twelve such meetings throughout the year, carefully planned and well attended, may do much to provide the general body of workers with practical help. Church school magazines and pamphlets offer rich suggestions for making these meetings more attractive and helpful. Where two or three churches are part of a charge or circuit, such meetings can often be planned as cooperative sessions for the workers of all the churches. This usually creates more enthusiasm and fellowship and reduces the demands on the time of ministers and other leaders. But, it cannot be stressed too much that careful advance planning and skillful conduct of such conferences are essential to continuing success.

(2) *Guided Reading.* Recent years have witnessed the production and distribution of a vast amount of literature that will be helpful to the average worker in the local church. Here is a form of training that is not dependent upon meet-

ings or cooperation on the part of others. Any leader who is willing to spend some time in reading and study can begin further training at once. Usually ministers, superintendents, departmental leaders and board members are acquainted with some of this material and will help to make it available. Magazines published by the various denominations represent the most continuous and specific effort to provide month-by-month inspiration and guidance for all types of workers. Surely no church will deny to willing workers, either by neglect or indifference, this important form of training. Often these journals become more meaningful if a group of workers will read and study the materials together. An increasing number of leaflets, manuals, and bulletins provide help on innumerable aspects of church work. They are brief and practical and inexpensive.

An increasing number of churches are establishing workers' libraries. The initial list of books may be small, but eventually the available material for reading, study and reference may become quite extended and helpful. Denominational boards have available lists of books which local churches may use in building such libraries.

(3) *Individual and Group Conferences.* Many of the problems encountered by workers are highly individualistic. Their duties are specialized. Fortunate is the church in which it is possible for these individual workers to find someone with whom they may confer regarding their work. Frequently it is the minister; it may be the general superintendent; more often it will be an alert departmental leader, or it may be a more experienced teacher. Multitudes of churches have failed to provide such "helping teachers." Beginning teachers, youth counselors, and newly appointed adult leaders have been left pretty much on their own. Supervisors are urgently needed. The public school long ago discovered the value of such assistance and virtually no school is without some super-

visory leadership. As ministers become better trained in religious education and are led to see the unusual opportunity for significant leadership in this type of service, they may render great aid in their churches as educational supervisors. Specific guidance for ministers who will take such leadership seriously is now available. Churches of some size and educational vision are employing on part-time basis experienced leaders in the community to give supervisory assistance in some one or more of the departments. The great value of full-time professionally trained directors of religious education is to be found in their continuing supervisory assistance to the entire staff of workers in the local church.

The informal, frequently held departmental or group conference represents another way workers may get assistance. The workers with children, for instance, may form a co-operative group to study and plan their work together. They may or may not have the supervisory assistance just mentioned. But they stimulate each other, share their successes and failures, and together evaluate and plan the work from week to week. Undoubtedly more of this kind of informal leadership training is going on throughout the country than most of us realize. It is decidedly worth encouraging. One alert leader in such a group can make it highly successful.

(4) *Training Classes and Schools.* The conviction grows that the various forms of leadership training discussed above need to be supplemented by a more advanced and formal type of leadership education. Slowly Protestantism is developing the vision and determination to undertake long time and extensive plans for providing the church program with better qualified leaders. The last two or three decades have witnessed the extensive development of short term training classes in local churches and longer term denominational and interdenominational training schools for volunteer workers. Thousands of such schools have been held and have made a great

contribution. Yet they have merely touched the great body of workers, and there is slight indication that the churches have as yet determined that such schools will be made available to the great mass of workers.

The main advantages of such schools are that they have high standards with respect to the amount of time made available, the training required of the leaders, the resource material used, and the outside study required. Where inter-church schools are held it usually means inspiring fellowship, greater enthusiasm, larger resuorces with which to engage leaders and provide rich resource materials. It means, also, the possibility of having much more specialization in courses than would be otherwise possible.

Such classes and schools are provided on a graded basis, *First Series Courses* being on a quite elementary level and *Second Series Courses* of a more advanced nature. Leaders must be met where they are. The First Series Courses assist workers with limited background of training and experience. The time required, five fifty minute sessions, the elementary character of the textbooks used, and the type of outside work suggested enable them to give vital assistance to such workers. For those with more training and experience, the Second Series Courses offer a longer program, a minimum of ten sessions of fifty minutes each, with qualified instructors and more advanced resource materials. Fortunately this whole program has been developed cooperatively among the denominations and it is easily possible for churches, few or numerous, in large cities or in countrysides, to plan together for the holding of such classes and schools. In many instances laboratory and observation classes are provided. Summer schools, institutes and assemblies afford unusual opportunities for churches to send carefully selected workers for training of a specialized nature that they could not otherwise obtain. It would seem reasonable to expect Protestantism to set up these schools across the nation in such a way that there is within reach of *all* workers in local churches some such opportunity for training.

Conferences and Institutes.—An increasing number of conferences and institutes are being provided, both on a denominational and an interdenominational basis. While many of these are brief in time they serve to bring men and women and young people into stimulating and developmental meetings. That church that insists on having representation in community or regional gatherings of leaders in men and women's church work, in missionary conferences, institutes on stewardship or evangelism, is using a significant opportunity to train lay people for more effective service in the church. Youth institutes and conferences are likewise affording opportunity to supplement the inspiration and training of the local church by that which may come from larger and more representative gatherings. Frequently participation in such meetings is just the thing needed to arouse new enthusiasm or secure the commitment of indifferent people. In all likelihood the number, variety and values of such forms of training will be greatly increased in the near future.

Making Professional Leadership Available.—Is it possible to conceive of one or more professionally trained leaders being available to every considerable group of volunteer workers in local churches? Wherever a church becomes financially strong enough and educationally alert it usually can provide such leadership for its own workers. The number of churches employing directors is steadily increasing. Such leadership is usually justifying its costs. The question arises, how can such assistance become more universally available. The great majority of churches seem unable to secure such leadership. It usually is the small church with limited facilities and few workers that most needs assistance. It is unable alone to engage such leadership. The only remedy in sight

141

(short of the possibility of the union of several small churches to form one larger church) is to attempt to provide such leadership on a larger parish or an interchurch basis. Many denominations employ special workers on a state, conference, or synod area basis. During the past few decades there has been a marked increase in the formation of state, city, and county interchurch councils. These councils in many instances are employing trained leaders who devote their entire time in providing facilities for training workers. Such a plan makes available to the most limited church the combined resources of all. It would seem that in this way only can Protestantism secure what it so badly needs in its educational program, a measure of professional supervision. An unusual opportunity confronts the minister who will secure the training that will enable him actually to serve as the educational director of his own church program and to give outstanding leadership in the larger relationships just indicated.

Chapter XII

Christian Education in the Larger Community

The Community as Educator.—Christian nurture is a complex and continuous process. A wide variety of influences and agencies have a part in it. Many of the agencies and influences that affect the ideals and practices of the growing individual lie outside the direct control of the church. In fact, it is when we seriously consider the matter that we realize what a large proportion of the influences that mould character are unrelated to the church's program and how fragmentary and limited her program of nurture still is. This program must not only be extended and improved in quality, but must also be more effectively related to the activities of other character-building agencies.

Churches and individuals exist in communities. It is here that they have their roots in actual associations and activities. Church leaders are coming to realize more fully that this community life must be permeated with Christian ideals, that all the agencies and activities must be made more Christian if the people who live in the community are to become Christian. They realize that many factors in community life are working against the ends sought by the church. These agencies are frequently well organized with capable leadership and large financial resources.

On the other hand, it is gratifying to note the growth of organizations that are concerned with the welfare of the people of the community and whose purposes are in harmony with those of the church. These agencies are finding it possible and necessary to coordinate their forces. Cooperation among social, welfare, educational and philanthropic agencies has greatly increased in the past few decades. Many communities have some form of coordinating council that brings together all forces working for the good of the community for cooperative planning and activity. Governmental agencies are also reaching out through city and county units to serve people with an ever broadening range of services. We are discovering anew that "in unity there is strength." It is in the midst of such a community situation that children are growing into adolescence and from youth into adulthood. It is in such a situation that churches are attempting to do their work. Critics of the church contend that churches are among the divisive factors in community life. It must be admitted that there is some justification for this charge. But churches are also experiencing new interest and activity in cooperative endeavor.

The World-wide Ecumenical Movement.—Coincident with this growing cooperation in the local community, there is new interest throughout the world in Christian fellowship. This finds expression under the rather forbidding term, "ecumenicity," which means world-wide fellowship among Christians. It is one of the most encouraging aspects of church life today. It is taking tangible form in an organization called the World Council of Churches. It now embraces in its membership almost the entire world community of Christians except the Roman Catholics. While this organization is in its infancy, the spirit that motivates it is strong and is bound to grow rapidly and become very influential. Such a movement is providing a larger framework for the growing efforts in cooperative activity among churches in local areas.

Cooperation on the National Level.—Cooperative

church activity has gone on in this country for many years. The oldest forms of continued interchurch activity in America have been in the field of religious education. In the earliest days of the Sunday school movement workers in local churches came together for fellowship and common study. Such agencies as the American Sunday School Union, the International Sunday School Association, now known as the International Council of Religious Education, the Sunday School Council of Evangelical Denominations, the International Association of Daily Vacation Bible Schools, have long promoted practical forms of cooperative Christian education. State, county and city Sunday school organizations have been reorganized into councils of religious education and councils of churches. Their number is constantly increasing. Such councils arise from the growing conviction that certain forms of church work and Christian education can be forwarded better by cooperation than by individual denominations and local churches. Denominations cooperate through such agencies as the Federal Council of Churches of Christ in America, the International Council of Religious Education, the Home Missions Council, the Foreign Missions Council, and the United Council of Church Women. These agencies are providing increasing opportunities, leadership, and resource materials for churches to cooperate locally.

Church Cooperation in the Community.—If the ecumenical spirit is to be ultimately effective it must find full expression in local communities where individuals and churches live and serve. Fortunately such cooperation is greatly on the increase. There are several types of cooperation, including, (1) fellowship and worship, (2) church comity (cooperation in locating and building new churches), (3) church extension, that is, the extending of churches and church activities into frontier, unchurched areas, and (4) interchurch activity in the field of religious education.

Our primary concern here is with the growing program of cooperative religious education.

Among the activities in which the churches actively co-operate in Christian education are the following: (1) week day religious education, (2) daily vacation church schools, (3) leadership training, (4) youth fellowship and activity, (5) adult fellowship and action, and (6) the development of lesson outlines. These activities all concern the local church's program of Christian education. They are forms of religious instruction which should receive increasing attention.

Weekday Religious Education.—The limitations of the Sunday church school in time, equipment, and leadership have been discussed. The 'divorcement of the formal teaching of religion in connection with the public schools, while seemingly necessary in the development of our American public schools, places a heavy responsibility upon the home and the church. There is ample evidence that they are not adequately meeting this responsibility. In addition to whatever the church and home may do to extend and improve religious education, it is necessary to extend religious education in a formal sense into the week time. *More time must be made available for the religious nurture of children of elementary and secondary grades.* One hour a week on Sunday simply will not suffice. Furthermore, there is a growing conviction that it is both unfair to religion and to growing youth to have religion divorced so completely from the program of education society provides for them in the public schools.

For youth to be introduced to the culture by which they are surrounded, to have all the major interests of life interpreted to them, *with the exception of religion,* gives them a distorted interpretation of their society and the place of religion in it. For these two reasons primarily churches, especially Protestant churches, have been endeavoring to develop a plan of teaching religion in the week time without violating the principle of the separation of church and state. Numerous proposals are being advocated, and some experimentation in various forms is going on. But the most common and widely used plan of providing religious education in connection with the public schools is known as weekday religious education. This plan calls for the release or dismissal of children from the public schools voluntarily and upon the written request of their parents to attend classes in religion taught by a church or a group of cooperating churches. This plan does not "put religion into the public schools" but does put religion into the daily program and experience of the children. Along with reading, 'riting and 'rithmetic, they get a fourth "R"—religion. They thus get the impression that society by permitting such an arrangement, and the church people by providing such instruction, believe that religion is a real part of life. For over thirty years such programs have been experimented with. There are over 2,700 communities, small and large, offering such instruction, under varying plans, to an estimated two million school children, mostly in the elementary grades. Scarcely a state in the union is without some form of weekday religious education and many states have well developed, state-wide systems.

The Legality of Weekday Religious Instruction.—There are those, of course, who contend that such a form of cooperation is a violation of the principles of church and state cooperation, that it involves at least indirect financial support of religious instruction by taxation, that it really puts the state back of forcing children to attend classes in religion. But every test of the plan in the courts of the country has resulted in a decision affirming the legitimacy and legality of weekday religious instruction. The mounting volume of successful experience over the country testifies abundantly to its practicability. Ultimately some of the other plans advocated, such as, the development of a common, objective treatment of religion taught by the public school teachers for all school children supported by Catholics, Jews and Protestants alike or the treatment of spiritual values with no particular reference to religion may be found to be the solution. But to date nothing has been presented that seems to offer the same opportunity to "do something about the matter" *now* as does weekday religious education.

Experience to date has shown also that to be effective weekday religious instruction should be provided on a cooperative basis. Few churches are able to command the personnel and resources necessary to provide instruction on a basis comparable to that of the public schools. Inter-church cooperation alone can secure the consent of the school board to such a plan, provide suitable meeting places for the classes, secure a well trained teaching staff, and command the supervision necessary to keep the work on a level that will gain the respect of the children, parents, churches and public schools. Many see no future for weekday religious education except on the basis of thoroughgoing cooperation among the churches of the community. In some communities Catholics and Jews also share in such programs. The Department of Weekday Religious Education of the International Council of Religious Education and denominational board offices provide splendid guidance in planning for such schools and in choosing or building courses of study.[1]

Vacation Church Schools.—For an even longer time churches have been supplementing their Sunday programs with religious instruction in the summer time. *Vacation church schools represent the most immediate, accessible, wide-open opportunity for the churches to increase the amount of religious instruction children receive during the year.* Such a plan utilizes the free time of pupils, teachers, and buildings. It does not involve the problems of close correlation with the public schools. It comes at a time when there is a minimum of competition with other activities. Held for several hours a day, on successive days, it represents a continuous intensive form of religious instruction seldom found in any other way. Extensive experience testifies to its effectiveness. The only thing that stands in the way of the more extended development of this form of religious instruction is the indifference and lack of conviction and action on the part of the churches.

It must be admitted, however, that with the slowness of the churches in utilizing the free weeks of the summer, the public schools and other agencies are providing more and more activity for children and youth in the summer time. Short summer sessions are becoming a part of many public school programs. Camping, supervised play grounds, opportunity for nature study, the cultivation of hobbies are greatly on the increase. It is to the credit of the churches that they have set up a large number of camps for children and youth. Most of these additional activities, by whomever sponsored, are wholesome and superior forms of character development. The church should, of course, be concerned to have as many of them as can include some form of religious instruction and devotions in their programs.

Many denominations plan for the vacation church school as an integral part of the local church program. There are many ways in which the teaching force, curriculum, pastoral relations and financial support of the regular church school may be utilized in making the vacation school possible and effective. Denominational emphases and programs may be easily incorporated in the vacation school program. There are many distinct advantages in schools conducted on this basis.

While vacation church schools have been largely conducted by individual churches, it is possible that such work will become increasingly interdenominational in character. The churches will meet stronger competition to any form of vacation church school as other forms of summer activity become more numerous. Better teachers, materials, buildings and supervision will be required and may be best provided on a cooperative basis. Courses of study for such schools are now being produced by joint action on the part of several of the denominations. State, county and city councils will aid greatly in promotion and supervision of these schools.

Leadership Education.—One of the most continuous forms of cooperative religious education through the decades has been that of the training of lay leaders. As far back as 1818 church school workers in such cities as Baltimore, Boston, New York and Philadelphia, came together to form city Sunday school workers' conferences for fellowship and mutual helpfulness. Such associations were so successful that national organizations, first the American Sunday School Union, then the International Sunday School Association, the Sunday School Council of Evangelical Denominations, and now the International Council of Religious Education, came to function in the development and promotion of extensive teacher-training programs. One may well wonder what might have happened to the pioneering, struggling Sunday school movement if these leaders could not have gotten together frequently to encourage and aid one another.

Leadership training is an integral part and an inescapable responsibility of the local church program. There are forms of such training that can only, or at least best, be provided in the local situation. Often the training needed by workers relates to denominational objectives and materials. At times such training can best be provided in connection with on-going activities of the local church program. And yet in no phase of the growing program of religious education has there been more wholehearted and effective cooperation than in the field of leadership education. Guided by the ideals and standards of some of the denominations, the International Council of Religious Education has brought most of the denominations together to develop a common program of leadership training. Such cooperation has included the development of standards, the outlining of courses of study, the selection of approved texts, the determination of methods of accrediting schools, instructors and students, and general plans for promoting and supervising classes and schools. Workers in one church can attend an interdenominational school or one conducted by another denomination and find the work practically the same as that provided in their own church and denomination. Under this plan the combined resources of all the churches of the community are made available to the smallest and most limited church. Many of the specialized courses can be provided only as churches unite to secure instructors and other resources. In addition to schools and classes, conferences, rallies, institutes, summer schools and other means of leadership development may be planned cooperatively. Few elements in the modern program of religious education have provided the splendid opportunity for honest-to-goodness fellowship and cooperation as has leadership training. Such activity bids fair to be continued and extended. When a church has thought through to the forms of leadership training that may best be provided by the local church itself and those that may be undertaken on a cooperative basis, and has entered heartily into the provision of both forms, it may be said to have *a program of leadership education.*

Youth Fellowship and Activity.—Each young person must have a church home, a place where he "belongs," where he assumes the full responsibilities of membership. Most of the religious needs of young people will be met by the local church to which they belong. Most of the activities that promote the welfare of both the individual youth and his church will be carried forward on a denominational basis. Any suggestions looking toward more cooperative activity in the pages that follow are made with this consideration in mind. There is no necessity of choosing arbitrarily between local church and cooperative activities. Both should enter into the religious training of modern young people.

Young people find themselves in a world that is striving for greater unity. Cooperation among the agencies of society and among the nations of the world is tragically needed. Modern youth are inclined to be impatient with the excessive divisions they find among Protestants. They are thrown together daily in the schools, in clubs, and in other forms of community activity. Yet these young people find themselves broken into small and often ineffective groups in local churches. In their religious life they are isolated from the Christian youth of the same age in the community. For the most part they do not care greatly about the differences that distinguish one denomination from another. On the other hand they have a strong desire for increasing opportunity to share the fellowship and activity of groups similar to their own.

For young people to study the Bible and religion in common classes in connection with the high school, to enjoy the enthusiasm and fellowship of the total body of Christian youth in the community, to join in study of the great social problems of our day and to unite in some form of action to help solve them, to share in various forms of interchurch recreation, worship, camp life, and together to train themselves for leadership, these are some of the richest experiences young people may have and constitute some of the requirements of the religious life of the community if young people are to be challenged successfully by Christianity and the church. Some of these larger relationships will best be provided in denominational groups. Provision for such activities will in other cases be made by interdenominational agencies. The denominations themselves cooperate through the International Council of Religious Education in the United Christian Youth Movement. The suggestions and programs of this cooperative agency must find their way into the life and program of the young people in the local church and community. Such participation need not lessen but may greatly strengthen their loyalty to and service in their own local churches.

Adult Fellowship and Action.—Much the same case may be made for interchurch activities for adults. In addition to all that may be done in adult work in the local church, adults too need the inspiration and help that may be provided through some form of interchurch association. Part of such activity may be carried on within the program of the denomination, part of it may well be interdenominational in nature. One of the weaknesses of the Protestant approach to the many problems and needs of the community lies in the disunity or failure of the local churches to pool their numbers and resources for a united impact. One wonders what changes might be made in the direction of total community fellowship and applied Christianity if the total adult constituency of the Protestant churches could be mobilized for united action. That remains yet to be seen. Schools of religion, religious forums, adult camps, rallies and institutes, and ecumenical services of worship are among the activities that adults might engage in cooperatively. Such cooperative activities should always be integrated carefully with the adult program of the local church.

The great and important task of informing and forming public opinion on many issues of significance to the church and the kingdom needs to be accomplished within most communities. It will not always be possible for church people to come to unanimous agreement on these issues. Yet there is great need that study, conference, and action should be undertaken. This may occur on an interchurch basis as well as in the individual local church. The International Council of Religious Education and the Federal Council of Churches of Christ in America are attempting through such agencies as the United Christian Adult Movement and the Commission of a Just and Durable Peace to bring adult Christians to a more informed and livelier sense of their responsibility and opportunity. The United Council of Church Women and the united mission boards likewise afford guidance for cooperative study and action in the local community.

Responsibility for Promoting Interchurch Activity.— These then are some of the areas in which the program of religious education may be carried forward on an interdenominational basis. These are the activities that such a group as the Church Board of Education in the local church should consider and attempt to relate to their own program. Throughout this book an emphasis has been placed upon the unity of the educational program in the local church. The manner of relating this program to the growing interdenominational activity is a matter for careful consideration by the local board. Frequently such relationship has been left to chance. These interchurch activities, if properly related, need not destroy the essential unity of the local church program. Churches should likewise realize that in order to make their own work fully effective in many aspects they must participate in such community programs with greater seriousness and continuity and with larger financial support than has occurred to date. The growing program of cooperative religious education can never be effective without such cooperation. It is a *must* in Christian education, a *requirement* in the life of Protestantism in this country.

The Church in Cooperation with Other Agencies.— Reference was made earlier to the numerous agencies that are committed to some of the same ideals and goals which the church is seeking. There is growing cooperation among public, governmental, and private agencies responsible for social welfare, character building, and crime prevention. This is brought about by the complexity of community problems, the ineffectiveness of unrelated efforts, the limitations of financial resources, the increase in delinquency, and the better understanding of character development. There are also many forces, organized and unorganized, that are exerting influences that destroy character and nullify the work of the homes, schools, churches, and character-building agencies. Against these influences, until recently, constructive agencies have not been united. Today the churches are being awakened to the power of the forces arrayed against its purposes and to the resources to be found in the average community with which it may federate its activity. Many communities now have a council of social agencies, or a coordinating council or similar organization through which they are combining their total resources in dealing with such problems as poverty, unsanitary conditions, broken homes, juvenile delinquency, gambling, drunkenness, and similar evils. They likewise team up in providing better education, supervised playgrounds and parks, family welfare work, club and recreational facilities, better housing, and hospital and medical care for those in great need.

The church has a great stake in all these matters. She originated many forms of human service now commonly accepted in society. She has everything to gain by close association and wholehearted team work with such community agencies. She will need to inform herself with reference to the moral and spiritual values in the work of these groups. While the church inevitably stands as a moral critic of community life, she nevertheless must needs place at the disposal of those working in the community her own ideals and spiritual resources for the betterment of the conditions of community living. She in return will receive inestimable assistance in achieving her own particular goals. For instance, when workers in the various child and welfare agencies of one of our large cities discovered the summer-time possibilities of the vacation church schools for their children, their support aided in increasing by 400 per cent the number of vacation schools held one summer. In another community sales of alcoholic beverages to high school youth reached alarming proportions. Repeated efforts of individual agencies failed to relieve the situation. It was only when juvenile court officers, judges, high school authorities, club leaders, parent associations, and church workers combined their efforts that the situation was corrected almost overnight. There is every reason for public school leaders, church workers, parents, club directors, and welfare workers, all dealing at times with the same problems affecting the same children and youth, being in frequent conference and uniting in common action to serve the best interests of all agencies and all youth. The Protestant churches should study the various coordinating movements and develop a basic philosophy of relationship of church with state and community agencies. Such cooperation is just in its beginning, and experiments should help create a body of experience and guiding principles for the effective participation of the church in community planning for making the "abundant life" available for all people.

NOTES

Chapter I

1. *Christianity.* Rall, H. F. Scribner's. 1941. P. 7.
2. Ibid. P. 86.
3. *Christian Education Today.* International Council of Religious Education. 1940. Pp. 9, 10.
4. *The Local Church.* Bevan, A. J. Abingdon Press. 1937. P. 20.
5. Ibid. Pp. 5, 6.

Chapter II

1. *The Educational Work of the Church.* Harner, N. C. Abingdon Press. 1939. P. 20.
2. *Education for World-Mindedness.* Murphy, A. J. Abingdon Press. 1940. Pp. 46, 47.

Chapter III

1. For the detailed study of special methods of teaching-leadership see:
   McKibben, F. M. *Improving Your Teaching.* Judson Press. 1934.
   McLester, F. C. *Preaching in the Church School.* Cokesbury Press. 1940.
   Rogers, W. L. and Vieth, P. H. *Visual Aids in the Church.* Christian Education Press. 1946.
   Smith, R. S. *New Trails for Christian Teachers.* Westminster Press. 1934.

Chapter IV

1. This list is taken from *The Methodist Discipline.* Methodist Publishing House. 1944. Pp. 187-188, as representative of one of the denominations. Readers are urged to secure from their own denominational headquarters literature descriptive of the specific forms of organization recommended for Christian education in their local churches.
2. Practically all denominations have helpful manuals describing in detail their plan of organization for each age group.
3. *The Methodist Discipline.* P. 183.

Chapter VI

1. Matt. 28:19.
2. Requests to denominational missionary and educational boards will bring lists of a growing body of helpful visualized material.

Chapter VIII

1. These journals are representative of the kind of literature now made available by the various denominations.

Chapter X

1. Published by The Methodist Publishing House.
2. *The Family Lives Its Religion*. Wieman, R. W. Harpers. 1941. P. 16.
3. See also Fallow, W., *The Modern Parent and the Teaching Church*. Macmillan. 1947: a most suggestive treatment of the home and church.
4. Readers are urged to canvass the literature made available, not only by their own denominational educational boards and publishing houses, but also by other church and independent publishers.

Chapter XI

1. Ministers are urged to consult:
   F. A. Lindhorst. *The Minister Teaches Religion*. Abingdon-Cokesbury. 1945.
   F. M. McKibben. *Improving Religious Education Through Supervision*. 1931. Abingdon.

Chapter XII

1. Those interested in further study of these schools should secure literature from their own church boards and
   Bulletin 601. The Week Day Church School, International Council of Religious Education.
   Bulletin 620. Choosing a Course of Study for the Week Day Church School. International Council of Religious Education.